# The New York Book of Coffee and Cake

# The New York Book o

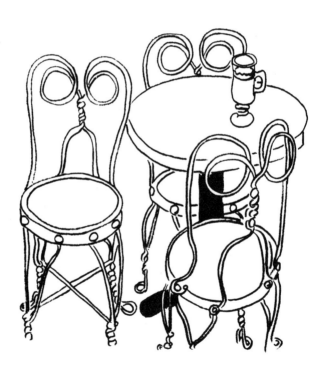

# Coffee and Cake

## BO NILES AND VERONICA MCNIFF

*Illustrations by Susan Colgan*

CITY & COMPANY

NEW YORK

City & Company
22 West 23rd Street
New York, NY 10010

Printed in the United States of America

Design by Leah Lococo

Library of Congress Cataloging-in-Publication Data is available upon request.

ISBN 1-885492-20-0
First Edition

PUBLISHER'S NOTE: Neither City & Company nor the authors
have any interest, financial or personal, in the venues listed in this book. No fees
were paid or services rendered in exchange for inclusion in these pages.

Please also note that every effort was made to ensure that
information regarding addresses, phone numbers, and hours, was accurate
and up-to-date at the time of publication.

# Contents

# Coffee, Conversation, & Culture

## Coffee on the Run

## Old-time Coffeehouses & Pasticcerias

## Franchises & Chains

## Coffee at Retail/Mail Order

# A Stimulating Sip

*Coffee "heals the stomach, makes the genius quicker, relieves the memory, revives the sad, and cheers the spirits... ."*

OF ALL BEVERAGES, none is as chameleon in its comforts as coffee. Be it a cardboard cup of joe-to-go or a dainty demitasse of barely sweetened espresso, coffee awakens us at dawn, perks us up during the morning or afternoon doldrums, and finishes off a lunch or dinner with elan. It activates the imagination and galvanizes conversation. Coffee, quite simply, revs our engines and keeps us going throughout the day—and into the wee small hours as well.

Whether you fly solo into one of the myriad stand-up bars around town or hang out with a friend on a comfy street-sofa in an ad-hoc coffeehouse, this bracing brew will excite and invigorate body and soul. Add a delicious muffin, cake, or pastry, and you're off and running.

We know. We were.

BO NILES & VERONICA MCNIFF

# A Brief History of Coffee

COFFEE'S ORIGINS CAN BE TRACED to Ethiopia and a local legend describing a simple goatherd who found his charges gamboling in the vicinity of a shrub bearing bright red berries. Tasting the berries, the goatherd was startled that he, too, felt a heightened sense of awareness and energy. He gathered the berries and transported them to a nearby monastery. The monks boiled the berries, drew off the liquid, and got into the habit of imbibing it to enable them to remain alert during prayers.

From Ethiopia, coffee beans were carried across the Red Sea to Arabia. It was the Arabs who removed the seeds from the berries, roasted and ground them, and then added boiling water to create "Qahwah," the precursor of the beverage we know today.

By the mid-17th century, an infatuation with coffee had spread throughout Europe. Coffeehouses sprang up by the thousands in response to its burgeoning popularity. Then, as now, one could find a cup of coffee, and an animated cultural or political discussion in progress, on virtually every corner of every major metropolis.

In the American Colonies, coffeehouses became the centers of radical political activity. It was there where patriots congregated to discuss, and vote on, the various measures which ultimately led up to the American Revolution. George Washington celebrated his inauguration, in April, 1789, at the Merchants Coffee House at the corner of Water and Wall Streets in New York City.

# Where to Go for Coffee and Cake

THE NEW YORK COFFEE HOUSE enjoyed a renaissance during the 1950s and '60s, when maverick poets, artists, musicians, and liberal-minded free-thinkers gathered in the pasticcerias opened by Italians some 50 years earlier. Coffeehouses along MacDougal and Bleecker Streets, near New York University in Greenwich Village, mimicked those in Little Italy in style, if not in substance, offering a place to hang out all day and late into the night, when jug bands vied with jazz, bluegrass with ballads, poetry with politics, and beatniks with hippies. Coffee fueled every debate. Today, the atmosphere might be less revolutionary in tone, but the old-time coffeehouses and pasticcerias are still going strong, pulling in a genial crowd that crosses generations.

Newer venues, both downtown and uptown, are serving up a generous mix of strong coffee and scintillating conversation—with some of the most delicious cakes and pastries you can imagine. There is no sense of rush, so you can linger as long as you like, alone or with a friend. Some spots, especially on the Upper East Side, bespeak a certain tamed gentility, while places clustered in the Flatiron District, in the Villages, and the southern end of Manhattan—are cozy meccas for the funky and far-out. Downtown, too, is where you'll find coffee, culture, and more. As in the Beat Generation era, painters, poets, writers, and performance artists show off their stuff in the wee hours; some places stay open as long as the action goes on—all night if anyone's still around.

As might be expected, most of the sleekest joe-to-go bars cluster in faster-track city zones such as Midtown East and West, where high-rise workaholics fuel and re-fuel on quick shots of espresso or macchiato, plus a megamuffin or brownie for an engine-gunning sugar fix. Most of the bars offer perch-at counters for a quick scan of the news, in print or on TV. The chains are democratic; they're literally everywhere, in virtually every neighborhood around town.

There are hundreds of coffee places in New York. We confess we did not take in every single one—but we culled the best and the most convenient. We've gathered our finds in chapters based on coffee-to-stay or joe-to-go. Turn to the index at the back to cross-reference your search by neighborhood. New places are opening every week. At press time, we discovered more we could not include. The choice seems limitless. It's all a matter of taste—and time. Whatever and whenever your inclination, there's a brew for you. Enjoy.

## What Bean's for You?

COFFEE BEANS, actually pairs of seeds extracted from the flesh of a red fruit called a "cherry," are green when harvested and hulled. There are basically two types of beans. Robustas are a lesser-quality bean, primarily used for commercial-grade coffees ground and packed in cans; they have double to quadruple the amount of caffeine as arabicas, the higher-quality bean which is typically sold, and packed, whole. Arabicas are the beans used for espresso and cappuccino (and their variations) served in most of the venues in this book. Beans are labeled with their country of origin and, occasionally, with their plantation. The degree of roast also appears on the label: Italian, for example, is the darkest, or deepest, roast; Colombian, the lightest.

The roasting process distinguishes the type of coffee bean you will find displayed in barrels and bags around town. The longer the beans are roasted, the darker they become. Roasting preserves the natural oils in the bean.

Skilled roasters roast beans in small batches. Like wine making, roasting remains an art determined by the duration of the roasting process at a given temperature. The various roasts are:

*Columbian Roast:* Beans roast at about 440 degrees and caramelize just before burning.

*Vienna Roast:* At 460 degrees, the beans begin to burn and develop body and a hint of smokiness.

*French Roast:* A full burn at 480 degrees maximizes the bold flavor of the bean that is favored in France.

*Italian Roast:* This 500-degree roast is the darkest of all, producing oily beans with an ebony hue and sharp tang; Italian roasts are those used, naturally enough, for espresso.

The longer coffee is roasted, the lighter the beans weigh because so much moisture is expelled in the process. Hence, dark roasts tend to cost more per pound. Commercial coffees (almost all of these are robustas) are lightly roasted; when packaged by weight, fewer beans are needed per pound. So-called organic coffees are those produced without the introduction of chemicals or pesticides; three years of a chemical-free harvest are required before a farm can receive certification that its beans are organic.

Decaffeinated coffees submit to one of two processes to remove as much caffeine as possible. Both occur before roasting. In chemical processing, a solvent called methylene chloride is added to water to absorb the caffeine; once the caffeine has been drawn out of the beans, the solvent is removed from the water. The water retains flavors, though, which are then reabsorbed by the beans. The water process, also called Swiss Water Decaffeinated Process, begins by soaking green beans in water in which the special flavor elements have already been introduced. The caffeine is absorbed into the water, leaving the aromatic oils and flavors of the beans intact.

Coffees may be flavored during and after roasting. Roasted chicory root, for example, is used to flavor New Orleans-style coffee. Sugar based syrups and aromatic oils, such as the popular hazelnut, may also be added.

## Brewing Coffee at Home

WITH A COFFEE BAR ON VIRTUALLY EVERY CORNER of this city, who needs to brew up a cup at home? We all do. To make the perfect cup, a little information and a few ground rules apply. The components are simple: beans roasted and ground to your liking and a favorite coffeemaker.

Coffee is ground to different grinds. The size of the granule is dictated by the type of coffeemaker you will use.

*Coarse Grind:* These large granules suit the French press or plunger and percolator.

*Medium Grind:* Similar in texture to granulated sugar, medium grinds are used with vacuum-drip coffeemakers.

*Fine Grind:* With a grainy texture similar to cornmeal, fine grinds are reserved for espresso machines as well as the drip and infusion methods.

The drip and infusion methods are those that roasters recommend to produce a smooth, full, rich cup of coffee; they feel that because percolators boil the coffee and run the liquid repeatedly through the grounds, percolator coffee tastes too bitter. (Water for coffee, in fact, unlike that for tea, should never be sustained at a roiling boil.) Measuring coffee is a matter of taste. While a ratio of two level teaspoons of ground coffee per five ounces of water is suggested by some roasters, you may prefer a stronger brew.

*Drip method:* Place filter in cone and position over heatproof vessel or mug. Heap freshly ground coffee to measure into filter. (Filters are made of bleached or unbleached papers; an alternative is a gold-plated metal mesh filter which lasts indefinitely.) To brew, bring water just to a boil. Pour over grounds to moisten them. Wait a moment; add rest of water. Remove cone. Discard filter. Pour coffee. Note: For automatic drip coffeemakers, follow manufacturer's instructions.

*Infusion method:* Spoon freshly ground coffee into French press or plunger. Pour just-boiled water over grounds. Stir grounds, then steep for three to five minutes. Press plunger to bottom. Pour coffee.

Because of their propensity to absorb flavors, beans, once opened to the air, can become stale within a week. Purchase only as much as you can drink in that week; keep the beans sealed in their airtight poly-lined bag in the freezer; remove and grind the amount you need at the moment you wish to brew up a cup or a pot, to preserve flavor and freshness. Be sure to keep all your coffee equipment clean. Oils can turn rancid and impart a bitter flavor to the beans—and the brew.

Coffee is best when drunk as soon as it is brewed. Ideally, you should not try to conserve it. If you must, transfer coffee into a thermos or so-called integrated vacuum pitcher. It will hold for a couple of hours.

# Reading the Menu

## ESPRESSO

Steam, forced under pressure through finely ground beans, results in a bracing brew. Although strong, a shot of espresso contains half the caffeine of a cup of American coffee. Typically taken black, or with sugar.

## CAFFE MACCHIATO

Espresso barely lightened with a drop of steamed milk.

## CAPPUCCINO

Espresso topped with steamed milk in a ratio of one-third espresso, on-third steamed milk liquid, one-third milky froth. Name derives from the color of the robes worn by Italian Capuchin monks.

## CAFFE LATTE

Espresso poured in equal parts with steamed milk, then topped off with a dollop of foamed milk.

## CAFE AU LAIT

Espresso, or French Roast coffee, poured and stirred in equal parts with hot milk. Many French cafes serve cafe au lait in large bowls rather than in cups.

## CAFFE MOCHA

Hot chocolate energized with a shot of espresso.

# Coffee
# Conversation &
# Culture

# Agata & Valentina

1505 First Ave. at 79th St. ∼ 452-0694

*Monday through Friday 9 A.M. to 9:30 A.M.;*
*Saturday and Sunday 9 A.M. to 8:30 P.M.*

AGATA & VALENTINA, named after the wife and daughter of one of the Italian owners, is packed with imported and prepared-on-the-premises food treats. For coffee, enter by the 79th Street door and walk up to the Espresso bar, handsomely built of unglazed terra-cotta, its "roof" tiled in the Roman style. While you can expect the coffee to be good (the house blends Sumatra, Colombian, Costa Rican, and Brazilian, and two flavored coffees are offered daily), rejoice in the abundant sweets. Handsome Italian-painted cake-stands display goodies like fogliatelle, apple crumble, Linzer torte, lemon squares, and triple-chocolate chunk cookies. Squads of glass jars offer variations on the biscotti theme. Sorbetti and gelati can be ordered packed or by the cone.

# Amir's

2911-A Broadway bet. 113th and 114th Sts. ∼ 749-7500

*Daily 11 A.M. to 11 P.M.*

AMIR'S GENIAL LITTLE CAFE, specializing in Middle Eastern foods, offers a pleasant respite from the crowds on Broadway and the rushing traffic pulsing around St. John's Cathedral and Columbia University. Everything here is bright and clean—cream tiles, pastel-flowered vinyl banquettes, and murals of houris, one a veiled danseuse, the other pouring water, painted onto the walls. The menu suggests Lebanese or American coffee, as well as the yogurt drinks beloved of the Levant. If you've always wanted to sample a Bird's Nest—pastry topped with pistachios and honey— here's your chance. Kenafi is shredded pastry with sweet cheese, pistachios and honey, and there's milk pudding with rose water.

## Basset Coffee & Tea Co.

123 W. Broadway at Duane St. ～ 349-1662
*Monday through Friday 7:30 A.M. to 8 P.M.;*
*Saturday 9 A.M. to 7:30 P.M.; Sunday 9 A.M. to 6 P.M.*

WELL, Lucy the Basset wasn't in when we were, but her presence can be felt everywhere in this genial, high-ceilinged TriBeCa hangout; just check out her palette-knife portrait, the recumbent faux-fido in the window, and mugs. A white-tiled dado, green wainscotting in the coffee bar, scuffed oak floors, and expansive windows create an informal surround for a dozen tables and green Naugy-padded chairs, where you can leaf through a paper or the current issue of *Java*, or work your way through Basset's specialty, a fresh-baked buttermilk biscuit (with or sans ham), or a fat wedge of walnut/sour cream breakfast cake, or a muffin from a selection that includes our favorite, "electric lemon." Basset's also sells over two dozen varieties of bean by the pound.

## Bazzini

339 Greenwich St. at Jay St.  ~  334-1200
*Monday through Friday 8 A.M. to 7 P.M.;*
*Saturday and Sunday 9:30 A.M. to 6 P.M.*

A ROYAL-BLUE CORRUGATED TIN ROOF trussed in red signals
the presence of this low-key dispensary of fine comestibles and coffees in the heart of TriBeCa that has been in business since 1886.
Coffee beans, about three dozen varieties, are packed and displayed
in small burlap-lined barrels; roll-top bags and scoops allow you to
measure out your own requirement. Of the beans, the Andes "with
a snap" and German Coffee Cake blends caught our fancy. Coffee
can be taken at one of a half-dozen tables in the windowed corner
of the loft-like space with a go-with such as turtle cheesecake,
American Beauty chocolate layer cake, butter cookies, or mud balls.
While munching, check out Bazzini's stuffed elephant head (it's also
on their logo, hanging onto a fat peanut) in the office alcove.

## Bean Bar

1516 First Ave. at 79th St.  ~  717-6392
*Monday through Thursday 6:30 A.M. to 11 P.M.;*
*Friday and Saturday 7 A.M. to Midnight; Sunday 7 A.M. to 11 P.M.*
24 W. 45th St. bet. Fifth and Sixth Aves.  ~  575-3889
*Monday through Friday 6:30 A.M. to 5:30 P.M.*

IN THE UPTOWN BEAN BAR'S inviting little coffee-and-cream
interior a pair of crimson plush armchairs occupy the window, and

sofas and chairs are carefully arranged en route to the counter, back left. Tree stumps inset with glass discs over coffee beans make novel tabletops. Studious types tuck themselves into corners, writing, while those of a less literary bent scan a TV which hangs rear right.

## *Bennie's*

321 Amsterdam Ave. at 75th St.  ~  874-3032
*Daily 11 A.M. to 10 P.M.*

A LONG SLICE OF MIRROR visually expands Bennie's Middle Eastern cafe restaurant, reflecting its white painted walls, service-able black chairs, butcher-block tables, and white and grey tile-clad columns. Along one wall, wine bottles are lined up like pigeons on a city roof. This is cheerful decor on a shoestring. Stop in on a morning when the owner is cooking in his stainless-steel kitchen area, open at back. As he throws in spices, savory/sweet aromas rise, evoking a sense of North Africa. Naturally, there are ethnic pastries like baclava, date and walnut confections, and borma stud-ded with pistachios; but there's also pecan tart, cheesecake, and German chocolate cake. Sit with your coffee and pastry, bring a newspaper, book, or friend; you'll be left in peace.

# Biblio's Bookstore & Cafe

317 Church St. bet. Canal and Lispenard Sts. ~ 334-6990

*Daily 8 A.M. to 8 P.M.*

OFFBEAT, OFFHAND, OFF THE BEATEN TRACK: Biblio's let's it all happen, whatever it is—as long as it relates to reading and writing. The espresso machine is a blackboard for magnetic poetry, and books there are, but this is not, repeat not, Barnes & Noble. The selection reveals the owners' individual and idiosyncratic pleasures and friendships with writers and poets—and with kids. Lower shelves are casually stocked just for children, who flock here on Saturday mornings. Two walls display an array of periodicals reflecting an ecumenical embrace. Although the cafe bills its closing as 8 P.M., it holds readings and performances often, so call for a flyer and see what's up, and at what time. You also can access Biblio's on Manhattan Cable Channel 17 "for a good dose of non-formatted television that features spoken and nonspoken types of banter and behavior." You heard it here.

# Big Cup Tea & Coffee House

228 Eighth Ave. bet. 21st and 22nd Sts. ~ 206-0059

*Monday through Thursday 7 A.M. to 2 A.M.; Friday 7 A.M. to 3 A.M.;
Saturday 8 A.M. to 3 A.M.; Sunday 8 A.M. to 2 A.M.*

THE CARTOON BIG CUP (held by an all-but-invisible, chubby-footed Little Fellow) that swings outside Chelsea's self-proclaimed "fierce new coffee house" signals a jolly introduction to its electric/eclectic loft-like interior. Day-glo colors slather every surface. Halogen octopi swim under the silvered-tin ceiling and highlight fat, kohl-outlined lavender amoeba-blooms, which float across an acid-green wall in the lounge area. Cozily furnished with thrift-shop sofas and chairs, the Big Cup is known for being laid back and for its Monday night bingo. Like the logo Cup, bakery goods are big here. Displayed in overflowing baskets, the vivid assortment of cakes, tarts, and pies includes All-American Cherry. Big Cup offers its spectrum of coffees in a miscellany of mugs and cups; a huge triple comes in, you guessed it, a big cup.

# The Cafe at the Angelika Film Center

18 W. Houston St. at Mercer St. ~ 995-1081
*Daily 10 A.M. until film closing*

A VAST, RAW-BONED SPACE, the cafe serves both as a pass-through and a pulse point to this avant-garde cineplex at the northern boundary of SoHo. You do not need to attend a film to stop off here, although, during the morning off-hours, the double-height room seems enormous, relieved only by a fancifully neon-braceleted crystal chandelier suspended from a painterly "sky" ceiling. Seating is functional—plastic and metal molded chairs, plus two modest, carpeted platforms at the perimeter of the room. During show times—and especially later in the day and in the evening, when crowds assemble—the place hops. Coffee and munchies such as brownies and muffins can be taken into the theaters. The Angelika promotes weekend brunch from 11 A.M. to 2 P.M.

# Cafe Bianco

1486 Second Ave. bet. 77th and 78th Sts. ～ 988-2655
*Monday through Friday 11 A.M. to 11 P.M.;*
*Saturday and Sunday 11 A.M. to 1 A.M.*

VISITING CAFFE BIANCO'S CHARMING GARDEN, hidden out back, you could imagine you're in Rome. The herringbone brick patio is enclosed by protective brownstones and prettified by trees that bow over trellis-topped walls. In this pocket of repose, 20-odd park tables and chairs permit caffe al fresco near a tiny fountain which burbles peacefully into a round pool. Espresso is served in tiny brown-glazed china cups or you may order caffe speciali, served with whipped cream, powdered chocolate, and cinnamon—the Russo is espresso with hot chocolate; the Irlandese, espresso with Bailey's Irish Cream.

# Cafe 59

BLOOMINGDALE'S
1000 Third Ave. bet. 59th and 60th Sts. ～ 705-2000
*Monday through Friday 10 A.M. to 8:30 P.M.;*
*Saturday 10 A.M. to 7 P.M.; Sunday 11 A.M. to 7 P.M.*

FOR SOME REASON, this street-access caffe bar is never crowded. Perhaps this is why it is so agreeable, placid even. Mahogany pan-elling and shelving, heavy marble counters and floors, and a damask-skirted central table add up to a solid, Viennese coffee-house feeling. Circular platters of croissants, tender brownies, and dainty muffins revolve around a column adjacent to the espresso machine, so select a bite as you await your jolt.

## Cafe Gitane

242 Mott St. bet. Houston and Prince Sts. ~ 334-9552
*Daily 9 A.M. to 11:30 P.M.*

BICYCLES LEAN CASUALLY against the pair of haphazardly repaired park benches that stand in front of this funky cafe just east of the art scene that is SoHo. As they sun themselves on the benches, a couple of old men from the neighborhood argue garrulously about whatever occurs to them. The front door decrees that the cafe is "ouvert aux visiteurs" and, inside, the gathering is truly catholic: visitors of all ages are granted equal space and time, even babies pulled up in strollers. A stainless-steel curve of a bar is banked with red Naugy-topped soda-fountain stools; after coffee, you can perpetuate your buzz with a Fireball from the bowl next to the cash register.

# Cafe Lalo

201 W. 83rd St. bet. Amsterdam Ave. and Broadway ∼ 496-6031
*Monday to Thursday 9 A.M. to 2 A.M.; Friday and Saturday 9 A.M. to 4 A.M.;*
*Sunday 9 A.M. to 2 A.M.*

CAFE LALO makes a specialty of coffee drinks topped with fresh whipped cream. Many of them are laced with liqueurs. But this is only the tip of the iceberg. Just take a look at the three-page menu of cakes, tarts, pastries, cannoli, cheesecakes, rugeleh, seasonal fruit pies, cookies, and biscotti which you can order with Italian ice cream and fresh berries. Not surprisingly, this appealing, relaxed spot is abuzz on weekends, especially in the wee hours when the young prevail. From the glassed-in balcony there's a handsome view of the attractive brownstones opposite. Bentwood chairs and marble tables emphasize the Central European ambiance; brick walls add warmth, as do antique elements and kitsch Italian glass.

# Cafe Mozart

70 W. 95th St. bet. Central Park West and Columbus Ave. ∼
678-7777
*Daily 11 A.M. to 11 P.M.*
CAFE MOZART UPTOWN
154 W. 70th St. bet. Broadway and Columbus Ave. ∼ 595-9797
*Daily 11 A.M. to 2 A.M.*

CAFE MOZART feels as if its been here forever. Maybe its the ruddy, vaguely Werkstatte chairs, the worn, warm buff walls, or the much-used woodgrain tables. Tapestry swags frame windows whose expanse of glass is delineated with a young Wolfgang. The walls are decorated with pictures of the composer, who seems to look askance as a generous dessert, Black Forest Cake, arrives. Taped music is, yes, you guessed it. In a corner, a writer corrects proofs as coffee arrives in a Melior French press. The West 70th Cafe Mozart focuses on desserts, supplemented with a light menu; at West 95th Street, the restaurant opens to an outdoor cafe. Both ventures resound to the harmonious strains of live classical music each evening between 9 P.M. and Midnight.

## Caffe Bacio

1223 Third Ave. bet. 70th and 71st Sts. ∼ 737-4730
*Monday through Friday 7 A.M. to 10 P.M.;*
*Saturday and Sunday 8 A.M. to 10 P.M.*

OUTSIDE, a wrought iron bench invites an iced cappuccino in the P.M. sun, filtered through lacy green gingko trees. Inside, light wood floors, well-worn dark-stain wood counters, and cream textured walls provide a quiet background for classic "kiss" photography—*bacio* means kiss in Italian. Food options here are for the size two set, with fat free-muffins and low-cal treats like French Twist cookies. For the rest of us, there are Silver Brook Kitchens bakery treats. Bunn brewed gourmet coffees await your order; beans in plexi cylinders behind the counter include Bacio's Blend.

## Caffe del Corso

19 W. 55th St. bet. Fifth and Sixth Aves. ∼ 957-1500
*Monday through Friday 7 A.M. to 8 P.M.; Saturday 8 A.M. to 5 P.M.*

CAFFE DEL CORSO has transcended its owners' expectations, so now this bright, fashionable little cafe/gastronomia is expanding. The cafe will remain up front in its present sunny incarnation where a lively take-out business sends a line-up out the door. Afternoons are quieter, the better to linger over espresso or cafe latte with fashionably miniature bites like the buttery palmiers or a diet-busting wedge of one of the creamy cakes. Your order arrives on tangerine-striped china, color-keyed to bakelite-handled cutlery. Take a moment to enjoy the pale and painterly effects that beguile the eye. A mural reminds one of Venice's Piazza San Marco; the ceiling offers glimpses of sky, wittily punctuated by Tovi bulbs.

## Caffe della Pace

48 E. 7th St. bet. First and Second Aves. ∼ 529-8024
*Sunday through Thursday Noon to 1 A.M.;*
*Friday and Saturday Noon to 2 A.M.*

ITALIAN POP SONGS ON THE SOUND SYSTEM establish the mood at this easygoing cafe-cum-student-center. Convenient to Cooper Union, the cafe is an amiable setting for art pieces which are handsomely, yet casually displayed throughout. The cafe nicely slices in two, with the coffee machines and cake bar, and busier tables, located across from the front door, and quieter tables through a gentle arch off to the left. Old-fashioned wrought iron railings set off raised areas in the bank of windows. Travertine or marble-topped tables are accented with tidy little arrangements of carnations and ferns. Servings of pies and cakes, by contrast, are huge. The robust apple crumb cake, for example, is stuffed with hearty chunks of fruit and dotted about with mega-sized "crumbs." Steamed milk with honey is an alternative to the espresso/cappuccino lineup.

## Caffe dell'Artista

46 Greenwich Ave. bet. 6th and 7th Sts. ~ 645-4431
*Sunday through Thursday 11 A.M. to 2 A.M.;*
*Friday and Saturday 11 A.M. to 3 A.M.*

IN BUSINESS ONLY THREE YEARS, the Caffe dell' Artista—with espresso-toned tin ceiling and coffee bar, and au lait walls—looks as if it has been a fixture on the Greenwich Village coffee house scene far longer. Its one-flight-up, floor-through location grants the cafe a pleasant vantage point on the street. Sun streams through a room-wide plate glass window onto a raised dais, which sets off a half-dozen tables and fosters cat-like contentment. A separate room at the back of the cafe and past the corrugated coffee bar is darker, moodier, more romantic—and there is a tiny appendix, a minuscule room containing only three tables where conversation might be as delicate and filigreed as the lace at its single window. As implied, the Caffe dell' Artista is also an art gallery; shows rotate monthly. Besides the typical dolci, there is a sublime plum torte— and three types of cheesecake: turtle, Italian, and strawberry.

# Caffe-Med

1268 Second Ave. bet. 66th and 67th Sts. ∼ 744-5370

*Daily Noon to Midnight*

CAFFE-MED'S SPARKLING BLUE-AND-WHITE AWNINGED, mahogany-and-glass windowed cafe could be a glossily casual Cannes bistro hangout. The impression is enhanced by a polyglot clientele drawn from around the Mediterranean basin. In the mood of sunnier climes, there's a patterned mosaic floor and a well-stocked bar with solid counters of reddish marble. Cream and russet woven bistro chairs are light enough to pull up around several tables if you take a bunch of friends. Recalling the Jazz Age, an African-American band jams on one segment of a wall-wrapping mural. On the other, a Toscanini look-alike lunges toward docile musicians. This all signifies that Caffe-Med presents live classical music midday; evenings, there's live jazz. Accompany this with Italian desserts, gelati, and a salad-y menu. Italian coffee flows, and in summer, tables spill outdoors.

# Caffe Tina

184 Prince St. bet. Sullivan and Thompson Sts. ∼ 925-9387

*Sunday through Thursday 9 A.M. to Midnight;*
*Friday and Saturday 9 A.M. to 2 A.M.*

MAHOGANY-FRAMED MIRROR PANELS, blush-tile floor, a small case with pastries, a handful of peach-toned marble-topped tables, a single ceiling fan: the appointments of this quintessentially modest-yet-elegant, family-run Italian cafe transport you straight to the heart of a neighborhood in an Italian city—Firenze, perhaps? Espresso or cappuccino is drawn into a chubby palm-warming cup decorated with the ubiquitous Lavazza logo. The signature Caffe Tina is topped with a dollop of whipped cream; espresso may be splashed with sambuco, anisette or amaretto. While sipping, admire the amusing pair of pictures—one's a hospitable pineapple—crafted of old lire, which were brought from the Old Country by manager Pino DiBartolo's brother, and hung with pride.

## Caffe Vivaldi

32 Jones St. bet. Bleecker and W. 4th Sts. ∼ 929-9384
*Daily 11 A.M. to 1 A.M.*

STEPPING INTO CAFFE VIVALDI is "like stepping back in time," as they say, but little did we know that the genial, antiqued look had been enhanced by New York's consummate movie director/stylist Woody Allen. All the portraits of composers that are ranked cheek-by-jowl on the cafe's brick walls were selected and framed for Woody's film, *Bullets Over Broadway*. The relaxed ambiance at the Caffe Vivaldi is graced by waves of soothing classical music, which wafts from the P.A. system. As the cafe counsels on its menu: "Where coffee is served, there is grace and splendor and friendship and happiness."

## Chez Laurence

245 Madison Ave. at 38th St. ∼ 683-0284
*Monday through Saturday 7 A.M. to 10 P.M.*

CHEZ LAURENCE is named after the owner, a baker and patissier from the Loire, and feels pleasantly *français* with its deep-set windows, pink walls, and old French theatrical posters and framed prints. Up to 25 different pastries are available here at any given time: six or seven varieties of danishes, half a dozen different muffins, and three or four kinds of croissants. Try the Pain Breton—a specialty—made with crushed almonds and dusted with sugar, or the robust creamy Napoleons. Ideally, try to avoid the early A.M. and lunchtime herd, select your pastry choice (tarte tatin, perhaps?) and settle in to enjoy your continental coffee and sweet.

## The City Bakery

22 E. 17th St. bet. Fifth Ave. and Broadway ∼ 366-1414
*Monday through Saturday 7:30 A.M. to 7 P.M.*

A ROW OF RONNEYBROOK FARM MILK BOTTLES and a vintage Rollfast bike greet you at the City Bakery's narrow downtown cafe. Inside, all declaims industrial chic: details include gasket-rimmed galvanized metal tubes to hold magazines, and pastry boxes, tied up with string, tic-tac-toed across the wall opposite the banquettes. City Bakery pats itself on the back for its reliance on fresh and organic ingredients. In the pastry case, our favorite cake winked EYES FOR YOU in chocolate sans serif print.

## Coffee Cuisine

543 LaGuardia Pl. bet. Bleecker and W. 3rd Sts. ~ 254-1662
*Monday through Friday 8 A.M. to 8 P.M.;*
*Saturday and Sunday 10 A.M. to 8 P.M.*

LOCATED JUST SOUTH OF WASHINGTON SQUARE PARK, Coffee Cuisine serves two purposes, to dispense brews, bakery goods, and gelati—and retail beans and teas. At the counter, reclaimed tractor seats swivel for ease of access. Ample tables and hardy oak office chairs are chummily corralled near the front door; more tables occupy a private alcove at the back. One wall is devoted to the display of the coffees and teas, plus filters and tins. Beans come from Gillies Coffee Co., purveyors of coffees for over 150 years. In warm weather, serious sippers can take the air on the outside deck furnished with French park tables and folding chairs. Muffins to consider include myriad permutations on bran.

## The Coffee Pot

350 W. 49th St. at Ninth Ave. ~ 265-3566
*Monday through Friday 8 A.M. to 11 P.M.;*
*Saturday 9 A.M. to Midnight; Sunday 9 A.M. to 11 P.M.*

THE FRIENDLY DECOR OF THE COFFEE POT centers on a faux living room set up smack in the middle of the cafe. The furniture arrangement consists of a low-slung loveseat and a chair, a coffee table (of course), and a side table piled with reading material. Off to the side, a pair of curtains hangs on the wall. Coffees are listed in bright markers right on the wall over the 49th Street window. Desserts, baked daily at Pietrasanta (a nearby restaurant under the same ownership), include their special white chocolate and chocolate mousse cake with Oreo crust. The array of cappuccini features a Razaccino, which is a "cappuccino with a raspberry zing." Chocolate lovers might like to try the snickerdoodle, hot chocolate made with steamed milk flavored with hazelnut.

## Coffee Times

2084 Broadway at 72nd St. ⌐ 724-3933
*Monday through Thursday 6:30 A.M. to 10 P.M.;*
*Friday and Saturday 7 A.M. to Midnight; Sunday 8 A.M. to 9 P.M.*
26 Broadway at Beaver St. ⌐ 747-9119
*Monday through Friday 6:30 A.M. to 5:30 P.M.*

THE DAY WE WERE PASSING the uptown Coffee Times, the baristas (professional dancers, it turned out) were having such a good time gyrating and twirling behind the counter that we had to go in and join the fun. The bench outside sports a Jackson Pollock-on-speed paint job; within, the walls are vigorously splashed yellow and white. Over the frosted steel counter pale green wall niches hold glass jars of beans to go. If you're seated at the black marble console table, a lean strip of mirror opposite will allow you to see who's coming along the sidewalk. Coffee drinks include the depth charge: brewed coffee reinforced with a double shot of espresso. Coffees of the day may include exotic one hundred percent Organic Gayo Mountain, or Ethiopian Sidamo.

## Columbus Bakery

474 Columbus Ave. bet. 82nd. and 83rd Sts. ～ 724-6880
*Monday through Friday 8 A.M. to 10 P.M.;*
*Saturday and Sunday 9 A.M. to 10 P.M.*

COLUMBUS BAKERY'S ROSE-ENTWINED MOSAIC FACADE, fronted by a raised deck sporting market umbrellas, is hard to miss. But wait until you see the broken-and-repieced mosaic tour de force indoors: i.e., a curved coffee bar, swirling with colorful fish and embedded with shattered plates à la Julian Schnabel. One wall is smudged a warm terra-cotta; freehand flowers and vines trail over the others. Twelve round tables match up with woven bistro chairs and flowering plants add a garden note. Huge sacks of Hitana flour underline the fact that baking takes place here round the clock. Sturdy racks of crusty breads, rolls, and foccacia will seduce your wallet, as your nostrils tingle to the fresh scent. Hard to resist pastries: berry clafouti, apple bread; sour cherry tunnels, or an absolutely decadent triangular brownie with walnuts.

## The Cream Puff

1388 Second Ave. bet. 71st and 72nd Sts. ～ 517-3920
*Monday through Friday 7:30 A.M. to 10 P.M.;*
*Saturday and Sunday 7:30 A.M. to 1 A.M.*

THE CREAM PUFF is the kind of tiny gem you hope to find in New York but expect to locate in the West Village. In the window, bracketed with wrought iron roses and painted with floral flourishes, a plant holder beckons, proffering cakes and cookies. It is eccentrically topped with a silver vase full of world-weary roses. Within, a vanilla-toned confection of trompe l'oeil effects dazzles the eye: landscapes, a round window, and marble panelling. Cherubs are everywhere you look. In season, fruit tartlets are overloaded with fresh berries, and there are three kinds of eclairs to tempt you.

## Cremcaffe Espresso Bar & Gelateria
65 Second Ave. bet. 3rd and 4th Sts. ～ 674-5255
*Sunday through Tuesday 9 A.M. to 1 A.M.; Wednesday through Friday 9 A.M. to 3 A.M.; Saturday 9 A.M. to 3 A.M.*

STEPPING INTO CREMCAFFE is like stepping onto the stage of a production of "Cav-and-Pag." To the left is the espresso bar and gelateria, and to the right are two raised areas in front of a mural of an Italian streetscape, complete with shuttered facades and tiled roofs. It's such a theatrically alluring scene that one expects to hear arias being sung as one sips a double espresso. A charming series of photographs of espresso cups lines the wall at the back of the room behind the "stages." Don't forget to nibble a panettone "crouton" set out on the saucer next to the tips jar, and, while you're at it, why not purchase some comfy little Baci; they cost $3 a packet.

# Cucina Vivolo

138 E. 74th St. bet. Park and Lexington Aves. ∼ 717-4700
*Monday through Saturday 8 A.M. to 9:30 P.M.*

THIS ELEGANT CAFE is the offspring of the next-door restaurant of the same name. The owners capitalized on the pleasant brownstone and tree-studded block with a floor-to-ceiling glass streetfront. The front tables, expectantly poised on marble floors, are oriented toward the view so that each visitor willy-nilly makes an entrance, and everyone can see and be seen. Fittingly, the cafe exudes a well-bred, scrupulously maintained blonde-and-beige chic. At the back, past the pastry and food display area, there's a light-filled atrium where white-napery'd tables are available. Nice with afternoon caffe: torta con fragole, lavished with cream.

# Dean & Deluca

One Wall St. Court at Pearl and Broad Sts. ∼ 514-7775
*Monday through Friday 7:30 A.M. to 5 P.M.*
DEAN & DELUCA PRINCE ST. CAFE
121 Prince St. bet. Wooster and Greene Sts. ∼ 254-8776
*Monday through Thursday 8 A.M. to 8 P.M.;*
*Friday and Saturday 8 A.M. to 9P.M.; Sunday 9 A.M. to 8 P.M.*
DEAN & DELUCA ESPRESSO
75 University Pl. bet. 9th and 10th Sts. ∼ 473-1908
*Monday through Thursday 8 A.M. to 10 P.M.;*
*Friday and Saturday 8 A.M. to 11 P.M.; Sunday 9 A.M. to 8 P.M.*

DEAN & DELUCA ESPRESSO
One Rockefeller Plaza bet. Fifth and Sixth Aves. ∼ 664-1363
*Monday through Friday 6:30 A.M. to 8 P.M.;*
*Saturday and Sunday 9 A.M. to 7 P.M.*
DEAN & DELUCA PARAMOUNT
235 W. 45 St. bet. Broadway and Eighth Ave. ∼ 869-6890
*Monday 7 A.M. to 8 P.M.; Tuesday through Friday 7 A.M. to Midnight;*
*Saturday 8 A.M. to Midnight; Sunday 8 A.M. to 7 P.M.*

EACH DEAN & DELUCA IS UNIQUE UNTO ITSELF, but all sub-scribe to the glamor of high-tech. Once the original emporium spun off its initial cafe on Prince and found it to be a success, others followed, each occupying an ever more distinctive and distinguished building and address. The Wall Street D&D, for example, is elegantly housed in the former Cocoa Exchange, a classic flatiron building. The Rock Plaza cafe is coolly sited near the skating rink. And the Paramount D&D is located just off the lobby of the Philippe Starck-designed hotel of the same name.

## A Different Bite at A Different Light
151 W. 19th St. bet. 6th and 7th Aves. ∼ 989-4850
*Daily 10 A.M. to Midnight*

LOCATED IN THE HEART OF CHELSEA, A Different Light Bookstore is the city's best-known source for gay and lesbian books, magazines, newspapers, cards and gifts. It's also the place to learn what's going on in the gay community. The cafe/bookstore offers poetry and book readings and film screenings so call for a listing of what's scheduled. One visits not only to be submerged in the city's alternative lifestyle scene, but also to nibble on delicious baked goods and relax in the bright, cheery windowed section in the front of the store. Sip coffee from their regular offerings and munch on linzer cookies or poppyseed poundcake slice.

## Eclair Pastry Shop
141 W. 72nd St. bet. Columbus Ave. and Broadway ~ 873-7700
*Monday through Thursday 7:30 A.M. to 9 P.M.;*
*Friday and Saturday 7:30 A.M. to 10 P.M.; Sunday 8 A.M. to 10 P.M.*

THE ECLAIR PASTRY SHOP and bakery opened on West 72nd Street in the 1950s. It still retains its original interior—a little run-down and exuding a melancholy Eastern European charm enjoyed by the elderly immigrant residents in the neighborhood. They filter past the bustling bakery section to find their accustomed tables in the hair salon-pink cafe at back, with its whimsical painted-tile accents, "modern" light fixtures that look like flattened spiders, comfortable banquettes, and white-clothed tables. The Viennese coffee mit schlag is delicious, as is chocolate "Opera cake," created at Rudolf Bing's command for the opening of the Metropolitan Opera.

## Eureka Joe

168 Fifth Ave. bet. 21st and 22nd Sts. ∼ 741-7500

*Monday through Friday 7 A.M. to 11 P.M.;*
*Saturday 9 A.M. to 11 P.M.; Sunday 10 A.M. to 6 P.M.*

AN ALL-BUT-INVISIBLE LOGO on its plate-glass facade belies Eureka Joe's roomy, comfy interior. A downtown edge and funky decor courtesy of the street and thrift shop could place the cafe in the East Village, except Eureka Joe is easily ten times the size of its counterparts in that part of town. The cafe bisects neatly into to-go and to-stay areas. The back, the apotheosis of shabby chic, is furnished with huge, squooshy club chairs and sofas all recently re-slipcovered. Faces formed of wire, a la Calder, hang on the walls, snow flakes dangle from the silvery tin ceiling, and stick-on mirrors extol both hot soups and PEACE, which is almost as good a combo as the mocha latte made with steamed chocolate milk—just one of almost two-dozen takes on joe that are the reason we shriek "Eureka!"

## Fifth Avenue Coffee Bar and Restaurant

389 Fifth Ave. bet. 36th and 37th Sts. ∼ 686-3560

*Monday through Friday 6:30 A.M. to 10 P.M.;*
*Saturday 7 A.M. to 9 P.M.; Sunday 8 A.M. to 8 P.M.*

YOU COULD EASILY WALK PAST the modest green canopy that simply says Fifth Avenue Coffee Shop, and that would be a pity. An atmosphere of Grecian sunshine and archaic charm seduces Manhattan denizens into a relaxed mood, especially on gray days when the uncluttered modern interior is most inviting. Suggestions of Greek columns are built into the apricot-hued walls, and the waist-high panelling with its Greek-key motif rail is picked out in a copper-patina green. Blond klismos-form chairs and copper-girdled tables furnish the space. Don't miss the baklava from an Astoria bakery, and cast an eye over generously sized treats such as macaroons dipped in chocolate, giant muffins, and huge hamantashen. As you leave, take note of the cash register encased in russet marble at the busy to-go counter.

## French Roast

458 Sixth Ave. at 11th St. ∼ 533-2233
*Daily 24 hours*

AS ADVERTISED, the French Roast maintains a high buzz all day—and all night, too. Of all the coffeehouses and espresso bars we visited, French Roast is the only one that serves round-the-clock. The "French" is supplied not only by the roast, but also by the ambiance. Black-and-white checkerboard linoleum, varnished beaded-board wainscoting, bentwood chairs, and a vintage sign announcing "La Maison de Cafe—Depot Ici—C'est Ca" are as allusive to the mood as the overheard intense, husky-voiced conversations. Beans to go are dispensed at the bar. Pastries include a mango charlotte, brioche bread pudding, lemon tartlette with raspberry couli, and hazelnut dacquoise.

# Heights Cafe

84 Montague St. at Hicks St.,
Brooklyn Heights, Brooklyn ∼ 718-625-5555
*Daily Noon to Midnight*

A RELAXED CALIFORNIA-STYLE sets the mood here at the
Heights Cafe, where upmarket Wall Street-types mingle with
neighborhood families. Warm and sunny colors—beach-sand
beige, apricot, and muted terra-cotta—are paired with the glowing
cherry and other good woods to establish the West Coast mood of
affluent informality. Frank Lloyd Wright-style lighting fixtures
throw a kindly glow on the sponged walls and on the busy tables
below, where patrons are seated in upholstered chairs. Italian coffees, and coffees laced with liqueurs, are made at the quirky piano-
shaped bar. Of the desserts, the hazelnut flan, served with an
espresso-maple sauce, is a customer favorite; there's also flourless
chocolate pecan cake, and Mississippi Mud Pie. If you like, you can
also enjoy your caffe and pastry outside shaded by a generous
awning striped in terra-cotta and toast.

# The Hungarian Pastry Shop

1030 Amsterdam Ave. bet. 110th and 111th Sts. ∼ 866-4230
*Monday through Friday 8 A.M. to 11:30 P.M.;*
*Saturday and Sunday 9 A.M. to 10.30 P.M.*

IF ANY CAFE IN NEW YORK CITY epitomizes college student life,
this is it. Enter on a cold day, when the windows are plumed with

steam, to find a warm and worn interior furnished with battered chairs and laminated tables jammed cheek-by-jowl. The darker L-shaped area at back seems to function as a kind of study hall, where computer screens glow like a swarm of electronic fireflies, and students slouch over laptops, or lie back in perilously tipped chairs gazing forlornly at the smoke-darkened ceiling. Those free to socialize or read for pleasure cluster closer to the counter, where orders are taken for gooey cream- or jam-laden pastries, generously sized to accommodate student appetites, and cream-laden coffee drinks. This is also a hangout for faculty families and neighborhood inhabitants, who otherwise would be hard-pressed to find coffee and cake. Ever-striving toward the heavens, the Cathedral of St. John the Divine looms across the street.

## The Indiana Market Cafe in the Joseph Papp Public Theater

425 Lafayette St. bet. 6th St. and Astor Pl. ～ 598-7100
*Tuesday through Sunday Noon to 9:30 P.M., or last intermission*

ONE OF NEW YORK'S BEST-KEPT SECRETS is the airy, echoey lobby cafe at the Public Theater. Owned and managed by the former Indiana Market on Second Avenue (now a catering company), the cafe serves up the requisite coffees and such treats as plain and chocolate cheesecake brownies, apple crumb and lemon squares, cinnamon/raisin tea cake and almond biscotti—and not only during theater hours. Two bright red banquettes sit in one of the west-facing windows; the column nearest the coffee bar is circled with a counter and high stools. Needless to say, when plays are on, the place is abuzz.

## Internet Cafe

82 E. 3rd St. bet. First and Second Aves. ∽ 614-0747
*Daily 11 A.M. to 2 A.M.*

WITH ELECTRICAL OUTLETS AND PHONE LINES at each table in this spare-yet-comfortable small cafe, you can grab a latte and set up a base to compose or create—or converse with the World Out There on your laptop. Two in-house computers can also be booted up for a nominal fee. For the "terminally" gifted, the cafe also has a video camera and a scanner, plus software programs such as Photoshop. For the merely literate, there are books (including a font guide, and "The Way Things Work," assorted periodicals and papers, and games such as Scrabble and chess. To stoke the brain cells, there's the usual lineup of coffees plus toothy sweets like brownies in four flavors. Partake of the cafe's Web "browse," e-mail, use of Word or Excel, or graphics programs. If you're a novice, you can book a training session in Internet or one in publishing on the Web. The Internet Cafe will send e-mail for you, too.

## Jane's

254 Greene St. bet. 8th St. and Waverly Pl. ~ 475-JANE

*Sunday through Tuesday 6:30 A.M. to 7 P.M.; Wednesday and Thursday*
*6:30 A.M. to 10:30 P.M.; Friday and Saturday 6:30 A.M. to Midnight*

PRIMARILY A STUDENT HANGOUT for next-door NYU, Jane's is
an unaffected and friendly place to plop a bookbag and stoke up on a
muffin washed down with a generous dose of caffeine. More than a
stopover, Jane's place is a command center for ten outdoor food-
and-juice carts which ply the parks. Here on Greene, though, the
effervescent Jane oversees the morning muffin crowd as well as an
evening clientele which drops by for music or poetry. Every
Thursday Jane features the Minetta Creek Band. Saturdays are devoted to comedy, Sundays to the Poet Tree Publishers Spotlight series.

## Joe Bar

2459 Broadway at 91st St. ~ 787-3684

*Monday through Thursday 7 A.M. to 9 P.M.; Friday 7 A.M. to 9 P.M.;*
*Saturday 8 A.M. to 11 P.M.; Sunday 8 A.M. to 9 P.M.*

YOU'LL SPOT THE SILVER-PAINTED CORNER COFFEE BAR from
afar—its whimsical black and white graphics look as if they were
created in a fit of coffee jitters. Surprisingly, the modest interior,
based on a black and white palette and given character by an
exposed brick wall, lends a wonderfully intimate sound quality—
you can speak at a normal pitch and still be heard. The lofty ceiling
with its acoustic tiles and an exposed brick wall probably account

for this fact, which is a bonus for the musicians who perform here on Friday and Saturday evenings. The photo exhibits are changed monthly. Check out the bulletin board, a microcosm of NYC life. Coffee options include a soy milk latte, and hefty fig bars, gingerbread, and chocolate raspberry crunch bars are among the edibles made fresh daily.

## Jonathan Morr Espresso Bar

1394 Sixth Ave. bet. 56th and 57th Sts. ～ 757-6677
*Monday through Friday 7 A.M. to 8 P.M.;*
*Saturday and Sunday 8 A.M. to 8 P.M.*
135 Greene St. bet. Houston and Prince Sts. ～ 260-6677
*Monday through Friday 8 A.M. to 11 P.M.;*
*Saturday and Sunday 9 A.M. to Midnight*

So, run this logo by us one more time:

```
J O N A    B
T H A N
M O R R    A
E S P R
E S S O    R
```

UPTOWN, the B A R is a sliver; downtown, a capacious loft-cum-art gallery. Both are paeans, as implied by the logo, to Jonathan's artistic sensibility (Morr's the mom). The stools uptown spring out from the wall like high-tech petals and the perch-at counter is slashed into an aggressive sawtooth. Polaroid transfers, by Claudio, of the stools, mugs, cups and saucers, et al., are clipped on the wall. Environmentally aware receptacles are labeled for recycling and waste. Of the sweets, check out the apple bar, pumpkin cheesecake, and sticky buns. Downtown, the spacious loft/B A R is dotted with trees and bisected with fluted Corinthian columns. Lots of officey/ airporty chairs and tables can be slumped into for schmoozing after checking out the art next door. A canted skylight striates sun at the back.

## La Boulangerie

49 E. 21st St. bet. Broadway and Park Ave. ～ 475-8582
*Monday through Friday 7:30 A.M. to 10 P.M.;*
*Saturday 7:30 A.M. to 6 P.M.; Sunday 8 A.M. to 5 P.M.*

IN BUSINESS FOR OVER A DOZEN YEARS, the bakery called La Boulangerie and its adjoining cafe have been an oasis on the eastern flank of the Flatiron District, predating and outliving many of the trendier restaurants that flash in and out as fast as a neighborhood photographer's strobe. One interior wall of the casual loft-like space is a giant mesh-gridded window that looks directly in upon the bakery racks. The decor of the cafe is in the honest service-with-a-smile mode. Deep window sills display slim baguettes, chubby "boules," and other breads overflowing their baskets to tempt passersby. La Boulangerie's cake list is hearty: sample mocha buttercream, for example, or chocolate ganache, lemon mousse or chocolate mousse cakes. Or nibble a delectable pastry such as the one called "Divorce," a choux pastry filled with both mocha and chocolate cream, dipped in mocha and chocolate. Cakes may be purchased whole or by the slice.

## Le Gamin Cafe

50 MacDougal St. bet. King and Prince Sts. ～ 254-4678
*Daily 8 A.M. to Midnight*

IN THE VILLAGE, MacDougal Street is lined with a number of old-time cafes adored by the bohemian (and neo-beat) set. Just south of Houston, though, MacdDougal ebbs into a quieter mode. Here you will find a single cafe, Le Gamin. With its sponged walls, French signs, and French accent, Le Gamin, which loosely translates as "mischievous one," could easily be in Paris. Mini-blackboards are chalked with specialties of the day. A long wall of periodicals encourages coffee drinkers to hang around, as does a stack of games. The sunny western window is a perfect spot, for instance, to hunker over backgammon or a jigsaw puzzle.

## La Linea East Village Cafe

15 First Ave. bet. 1st and 2nd Sts. ～ 777-1571
*Tuesday, Wednesday and Thursday 8 A.M. to 1 A.M.;*
*Friday and Saturday 9 A.M. to 4 A.M.;*
*Sunday and Monday 9 A.M. to Midnight*

LA LINEA is a distinctively coffee-and-art sort of place, its color-washed walls as painterly as any canvas. The colors evoke the bright hues of Van Gogh's Provence: sunflower yellow, cypress green, and sky blue. The gallery space behind the coffee bar is delineated by an exposed plywood subfloor painted poppy. Back here, pairs of low-slung chairs slipcovered in black cotton encourage relaxation. Art changes monthly; a pad and pencil are suspended for sign-ins or comments on the exhibitions. To find out which evenings music is scheduled, call—or just drop in to see what's on.

## Le Petit Cafe

453 W. 54th St. at Tenth Ave. ~ 974-8710
*Daily 8 A.M. to 5 P.M.*

JUST OFF TENTH AVE., Le Petit Cafe's modern facade, suggesting a wind-blown Hampton's dune fence rendered in steel, leans out into the street. The modestly furnished interior retains brownstone charm with a daffy and disarming admixture of Caribbean color and 1950s' Zeitgeist. The raw brick walls are painted white; the lower half is swimming pool aqua. There are simple tables and tubular metal chairs where you can imbibe coffee and your sweet treat. Unframed oil paintings on the wall contribute to the impro-vised but friendly feeling.

# Lexington Candy Shop

1226 Lexington Ave. at 83rd St. ~ 288-0057

*Monday through Saturday 7 A.M. to 7 P.M.; Sunday 9 A.M. to 6 P.M.;*
*Closed on Sunday during summer*

YOU KNOW THE LEXINGTON CANDY SHOP even if you don't, so to speak, since the Edward Hopper-like corner shop has appeared in many movies. The inside story is generic New York coffee shop, vaguely 1940s, with worn wood fixtures, green leatherette-upholstered wood booths, and pink laminate tables edged diner/retro-style with metal trim. Seated on a stool at the counter, you're served your order in familiar diner china, thick and comforting in the hand. As you look around, you'll notice all the framed movie star photos, signed by hopefuls not heard of since—and how much younger the ones you do recognize are in their pix: check out Robert Redford, Cousin Brucie, and Telly Savalas.

# Limbo

47 Ave. A bet. 3rd and 4th Sts. ~ 477-5271

*Monday through Thursday 8 A.M. to 1 A.M.; Friday 8 A.M. to 2 A.M.;*
*Saturday 9 A.M. to 2 A.M.; Sunday 9 A.M. to 1 A.M.*

HANGING OUT AT LIMBO is like hanging out in . . . limbo. Come in, sit down, crumble up a cranberry or blueberry-speckled angel food muffin, and sip a coffee of your choice in its Fiestaware cup or mug—and, once the buzz sets in, try your hand at a game of Scrabble or pore over a cinemag looped over a fat red hook on the central column. Limbo's decor is pleasingly spartan: diner-issue tables topped with boomerang-patterned Formica, wooden chairs cushioned in torn vinyl. Large sepia-tone photos are buttoned to the buttery walls and fragile-looking wire sculptures float from the ceiling. Huge green doors pivot open to the street in warm weather. At the back of the space a tiny cubbyhole welcomes intimate transactions. Limbo does a brisk business at night, with entertainment switching off from comedy to poetry to jazz. If you're wondering if the Force will be with you sometime soon, drop in for a reading of your Tarot cards with Betsy on Mondays or Thursdays; she starts at 8 P.M. and goes until whenever she feels like stopping.

## Marquet Patisserie

15 E. 12th St. bet. Fifth Ave. and University Pl. ~ 229-9313
*Monday through Friday 7:30 A.M. to 8 P.M.;*
*Saturday 8 A.M. to 8 P.M.*

A HINT OF AD HOC "ARCHITECTURE" adds a fillip to this cafe located across from the Cinema Village. The front of the room is capped with panels of sheet metal and plywood resting on tracks, and the long counter displaying the bakery goodies boasts a plywood base. Plywood panels also hang from tracks at the back, to discreetly shield the kitchen from view. Tiny halogen lights halo croissants and other breakfasty tasties, and an enormous baker's rack displays upended breads and brioches with singular flair. All cakes are works of art, as are the eclairs, individual tarts, and tiny truffles. Many pastries—all baked by Marquet in Brooklyn—are crafted, and iced as single servings; check out the toothsome wedges, especially of the mousse cakes.

# The Mezzanine Cafe at Barnes & Noble

2289 Broadway bet. 82nd and 83rd Sts. ∼ 362-8835
160 E. 54th St. bet. Lexington and Third Aves. ∼ 750-8033
675 Sixth Ave. bet. 21st and 22nd Sts. ∼ 727-1227
*Daily 9 A.M. to Midnight*

SO POPULAR HAVE THE B&N CAFES BECOME that on weekends you may find yourself waiting in line. No matter; you can skim through the book you just bought as you wait for table space. The clientele is as various, surprising, and interesting as the books that lie in wait on the miles of shelves, and the relaxed atmosphere is conducive to conversation and friendship. The coffee is Starbucks, and the busy baristas know what they're doing, so cappuccino comes with a deep, velvety pad of foam, through which to inhale the flavorful blends. Nor will a request for caffe latte decaf double short faze them. Foodstuff is robust and imaginative. Low-fat carrot-zucchini ginger loaf belies its calorie/health-conscious image, sweet potato-cranberry bread teases the palate, and almond-cherry tarts are sweet and sharp in pastry collars. Books, caffe, and sweet bites: read our lips!

# Milan Cafe & Coffee Bar

120 W. 23rd St. bet. Sixth and Seventh Aves. ~ 807-1801

*Monday through Thursday 7:30 A.M. to 10 P.M.; Friday 7:30 A.M. to 11 P.M.; Saturday 9 A.M. to 11 P.M.; Sunday 9 A.M. to 10 P.M.*

RUSTIC OF TEMPERAMENT, the Milan is a cozy newcomer to the neighborhood that harbors the Big Boys: Bed, Bath & Beyond, Today's Man, and Barnes & Noble, among others. Mismatched striped pine furnishings collegially mix under fluttering white grommeted banners tethered to guy-wires pulled taut in rows below the high ceiling. Stucco walls, an inlaid mosaic counter, and wrought iron rooster-topped hooks add to the cosmopolitan-meets-country ambiance. Coffee is served in comfortably chunky cups and saucers. Sweets include an orange cheesecake as well as chocolate-dipped biscotti.

# Miss Grimbles Cafe & Espresso Bar

312 Columbus Ave. bet. 74th and 75th Sts. ~ 595-CAKE

*Monday through Thursday 7 A.M. to 11 P.M.; Friday 7 A.M. to 1 A.M.; Saturday 8 A.M. to 1 A.M.; Sunday 8 A.M. to 11 P.M.*

MISS GRIMBLES ORIGINATED as a wholesale bakery specializing in cheesecake; as a cafe, Miss Grimbles indeed offers cheesecakes galore, plus companionable coffee drinks, and specializes in the kind of desserts that make little kids and teenagers' eyes grow wide. If chocolate's your downfall, chocolate espresso almondine cake may be the way you want to go. Espresso-soaked genoise cake is sandwiched with buttercream filling iced with chocolate, and liberally sprinkled with crunchy sweet almonds. This ensures you will spend a sleepless night counting your calories over and over. And now there's Miss Grimbles in a music mood, too: jazz or Caribbean sounds can be heard every night save Tuesday and Saturday.

## The Muffin Man

1638 Third Ave. bet. 91st and 92nd Sts. ⁓ 987-2404
171 First Ave. and First St.
Park Slope, Brooklyn ⁓ 718-768-2022
*Daily 6:30 A.M. to 10 P.M.*

SUPPLIED BY Connecticut Muffin Company's New York City bakery, both the Manhattan and Brooklyn venues offer moist and luxurious cakes by the slice, and compact, weighty muffins that you can really sink your teeth into. The Third Avenue location is a roomy, sociable spot designed by one of the company's partners. Hand carved "art brut" wood seats represent recognizable New York types such as a zaftig lipsticked and gold-braceleted matron, a '50s hunk with a pleased smirk on his lips, a Bob Dylanish guy with a Harley cap, plus two "character" chairs for kids. Quirky wood tables carved by the same hand pose on tiptoe on the apricot tile floor. Mellow yellow walls, a coffered white ceiling, and a storewide counter where you can belly up to the goodies complete the picture. Fresh flowers in pots add a nice touch, and French doors open onto the street. The outside deck at the Park Slope store is beloved by the neighborhood.

## Munson Diner

600 W. 49th St. at 11th Ave. ～ 246-0964

*Daily 24 hours.*

IN AN AREA punctuated by car dealerships and repair shops, you'll come across a true 40s stainless-steel diner. Venturing inside, you almost expect Bogie to turn around on one of the chunky revolving counter stools and fix you with a hard stare. The orange counters and tables are clean but scuffed with use, and behind the former, white-clad employees bustle at the sizzling griddle and dispense coffee from a capacious commercial urn. The stainless-steel panels behind the counter are designed with sunray patterns that catch the flinty New York light from the unpromising neighborhood outside; above, bright blue swirled laminated panels intersect Scrabble-style lists of eats. Take a booth up front, order the "house" coffee, a Colombian blend, and settle down to read the *Taxi News* (it even has pinups). Yes, this is where all those cabbies hang out on wet evenings. . .

## 9 Coffee House

110 St. Mark's Pl. bet. First Ave. and Ave. A ～ 982-7129

*Monday through Thursday 10 A.M. to 1 A.M.;*
*Friday and Saturday 10 A.M. to 2 A.M.; Sunday 10 A.M. to Midnight*

EVERYTHING ABOUT 9 IS HIGH-GLOSS: the lacquered sienna-brick walls; the shiny tables and chairs—each a boldly executed work of art painted with squiggles, dots, chevrons and the like; and the coffee bar itself, which, with its rays and bullseye, is also a muralist's delight. Each chair back has been cut with a fanciful crown: a sawtooth, a skyline, droll bubbles. Even the bookcase at the back is sculpted and given a sheen. Conversation's a shimmering thing, too, apparent from the throngs who cluster here, especially on weekends and at night when the entire St. Mark's strip pulsates from east of Astor Place straight on through to Avenue A.

## No Bar Cafe

432 E. 9th St. bet. First Ave. and Ave. A ~ 477-2877

*Monday through Friday Noon to Midnight;*
*Saturday and Sunday Noon to 1 A.M.*

IN KEEPING WITH ITS EMPHASIS ON ANONYMITY, the No Bar—at the far end of East 9th's "collectibles" row, near Tompkins Square—is a pure example of what used to be called "urban decay," but might be updated to "virtual streetscape": glazed-over cracked-plaster walls; wainscotting fabricated from odd bits of woodsy flotsam and jetsam; doors rubbed raw to expose steel that had been concealed under layers of paint; mismatched tables and chairs. Windows dressed with knotted black curtains overlook a garden at the back. A resident art show is changed on a monthly basis. Coffees here can be tempered with soy milk. Steamed milk, vanilla chaud (steamed with a hint of vanilla), cafe au lait, and cafe latte are served in bowls. For a new take on sweets, the dessert lineup is rounded out with French-style crepes. Wednesday, Friday, and Saturday evenings are dedicated to North African music or blues.

# Once Upon a Tart

135 Sullivan St. bet. W. Houston and Prince Sts. ～ 387-8869

*Monday through Friday 7 A.M. to 8 P.M.;*
*Saturday 8 A.M. to 8 P.M.; Sunday 8 A.M. to 6 P.M.*

FIVE TIERS OF TARTS and other bakery goods displayed in the
window and a giant tart pan swinging from the awning prove irresistible to passersby in this quiet "suburb of SoHo." Being slightly
off the beaten path of the gallery scene (especially on weekends)
only adds to Once Upon's allure. A vintage photograph portrays
the shop as it was. A half-dozen minuscule tables and rubbed steel
chairs—with backs that evoke a cross between Gothic and Picket
Fence—compel intimacy. (Indeed, the circumference of one of the
muffins appears to rival that of a table top.) Hunker here with your
true love, or a newspaper—or both—and share a caffe and the
sugar fix guaranteed by the tart of your whim. If you're in a so-
called healthier frame of mind, the muffins have rambling names
that must be poesy to the ears of the organically inclined. To wit:
oatbran/apple/raisin. Scones include—for just-us-folks—straightforward Irish soda.

# *O*zzie's

136 Montague St. bet. Henry and Clinton Sts.,
Brooklyn Heights, Brooklyn ∾ 718-852-1553
*Sunday through Thursday 7 A.M. to 11 P.M.;*
*Friday and Saturday 7 A.M. to Midnight*
57 Seventh Ave. at Lincoln Pl.
Park Slope, Brooklyn ∾ 718-398-6695
*Daily 6 A.M. to Midnight*

EVERYONE IN PARK SLOPE knows Ozzie's, housed in a turn-of-the-century pharmacy and retaining much of its atmosphere and many of the old fixtures. Adopted by a young neighborhood set, it features live music—jazz or guitar by local musicians—on Wednesday nights. Now there's a new Ozzie's in Brooklyn Heights. Like the original, this one offers an eclectic assortment of coffee and tea collectibles—McCoy tea sets, 1950s coffee pots, cups and saucers, and other brew-related paraphernalia. The comfortable, relaxed space with natural wood floors and white-and-hunter green color scheme seats about thirty indoors at green marble cafe tables; on the patio, among flowering plants, there's seating for twenty or so more. Plenty of toothsome pastries are made for Ozzie's by specialty bakers. The store also sells close to thirty varieties of coffee beans, including organic beans such as Mocha Java and Costa Rica.

# Papi Luis Cafe and Queer Cultural Bastion
34 E. 2nd St. at Second Ave. ～ 473-5021
*Sunday through Thursday Noon to 1 A.M.;*
*Fridays and Saturdays Noon to 2 A.M.*

THIS COOL ALL-WHITE CAFE, named for a carwash in Puerto Rico, is, by day, a quiet place to sample a coffee. For browsers, there's a peninsula covered with stacks of magazines and a small case with books. Padded banquettes, slipcovered folding chairs, covered stools, and a sunny south window create a warm, welcoming environment. At night, the place starts to jive. Papi Luis calls itself "gay-friendly" and devotes themed evenings to gay and lesbian events. Here's the weekly breakdown: Monday: Bingo, with a drag queen as a caller. Tuesday: Videos, when young video artists introduce their new work. Wednesday: Poetry. Thursday: Open for parties. Anyone can host an event—just inquire. Friday and Saturday are "standard weekend" nights; Sunday's for lesbians.

# Paradise Cafe
139 Eighth Ave. bet. 17th and 18th Sts. ～ 647-0066
*Monday through Thursday and Sunday 6:30 A.M. to 10 P.M.;*
*Friday and Saturday 6:30 A.M. until Midnight.*

TWO BLOCKS SOUTH of the Joyce Theater on lower Eighth Avenue's restaurant row, Paradise Cafe stands out for its 6 P.M.-to-midnight "Happy Hour," when it offers a small cup of free coffee with the purchase of a slice of pie or piece of cake. Of the latter, the brownie cheesecake triple layer chocolate (Heaven) cake most eloquently spells out its sinfulness. Paradise is a soothing Eden in peachy hues: French doors open to the sidewalk so passersby can sniff the java and look in across to the pastry case displaying myriad muffins, cookies, and strudel. Chocolate-raspberry dip sticks are 25 cents apiece, five for $1.

## Patisserie J. Lanciani

271 W. 4th St. bet. Perry and 11th Sts.  ∼  929-0739
*Sunday and Monday 8 A.M. to 10 P.M.; Tuesday, Wednesday and Thursday
8 A.M. to 11 P.M.; Friday and Saturday 8 A.M. to Midnight*

TO ENTER THIS SUNNY and charming patisserie in the West Village, you must walk between two shoulder-high glass brick partitions which partially obscure the dazzling array of pastries featured in a storewide case before you. On either side of the entryway, and looking out through huge plate-glass windows to the streetscape, cluster a half-dozen vintage diner tables, their pale pink laminate tops accented with ridged steel bands. Fully cognizant of its charms, the patisserie proudly displays not art, but framed write-ups from *New York* magazine and other effusive sources. Of the two-dozen cakes (there are lots of tarts and truffles, too) on display, several for chocoholics stand out: Black Forest; a ganache, called "Blackout," an old-fashioned Boston cream pie; and a just-as-traditional chocolate layer cake.

# Pink Pony Cafe

174 Ludlow St. bet. Houston and Stanton Sts.
*Saturday through Thursday 10 A.M. to Midnight;*
*Friday and Saturday 10 A.M. to 4 A.M.*

MORE OF A HAPPENING THAN A CAFE, the Pink Pony is the sort of guileless, casual place where people sort of wander in and sort of hang out with whatever happens to be set out on the counter. The address is "probably 174 or maybe it's 176;" there's no telephone. A lounge area outfitted with a rattan sofa and chair dressed in bile-hued pseudo-provencal cotton links the coffee bar to a dusky play-room fitted-out with a half-size pool table, a Twilight Zone arcade game, some kiddie-tyke bikes and a ride 'em horsey—and an upright piano for when the mood strikes. At the front, improvised racks display a huge assortment of magazines; check out *Farm Pulp, Reptile & Amphibian, Optic Nerve Vol. 1,* or perhaps *Private Line,* the Journal of Inquiry into the Telephone System. Human skulls serve as bookends. At the Pink Pony, entertainment is occasional and serendipitous. A film? Some jazz? It all depends . . . By the way, palm readings are $5.

# Resume Cafe

150 Second Ave. bet. 9th and 10th Sts.  ∼  982-6194

*Sunday through Thursday 10 A.M. to Midnight;*

*Friday and Saturday 10 A.M. to 2 A.M.*

EVERY ONCE IN A WHILE, a place is invented for a reason that sets it apart from the run-of-the-mill. Resume Cafe is such a locale. As its business card states, the cafe is bipartisan: it honors coffee— and contacts. The brick wall is thick with resumes, neatly organized and pushpinned to the wall for inspection by the curious—and, one hopes, by headhunters and those from human-resources departments. Because of the nature of the neighborhood, resumes tend to concentrate on careers in the arts: writing, film production, acting, and fashion. One evening a week, Tim Haft, a writer on the subject of careers, makes himself available, for $10, to critique your resume and give counsel on how to pursue opportunities in your field. Accompany his wisdom with a profiterole or cappuccino cake—or maybe an espresso laced with sambuca.

# Rizzoli SoHo

454 W. Broadway bet. Prince and Spring Sts.  ∼  674-1616

*Monday through Saturday 10:30 A.M. to 9 P.M.; Sunday Noon to 7 P.M.*

THE LUSHLY CARPETED, library-like ambiance of Rizzoli SoHo is so inviting that one might long to linger here with a cup of coffee. And so one can. Ascend the stairs, past Dreams and Positive Thinking, and drift over to the window on the second floor. The snug bar located here makes its own hours, but usually opens around noon and dispenses coffee to a quartet of tables until 8 P.M. or so. The bar is convenient to a couple of alluring discount tables as well as to the Design and Photography selections—and to periodicals, some of which are piled on a counter in the window, so you can simultaneously scan a mag—*Metropolis,* say, or *Interview,* or *Bomb*—and check out the West Broadway stroll scene below. P.S. They say that this Rizzoli's is great for meeting people, too.

## Scharmann's

386 W. Broadway bet. Spring and Broome Sts. ∼ 219-2561
*Daily 10 A.M. to 9 P.M.*

SOHO MEETS *CASABLANCA* in this vast loft accented by a huge-fronded palm. Peachy walls drizzled with paint and the brush-washed floor are the backdrop for an amazing amalgam of ritzy/relaxed rococo furnishings that artfully evoke the Fontainbleaus of Miami and France. Let your antennae tell you where to seek repose; furniture styles are as eclectic as the clientele. You may choose, for instance, to recline upon a velvety chaise, tuck your feet up on a tufted sofa, plop onto a beanbag or squat on a furry footstool. Or invite a gang of pals to gather around a sensuously appointed banquet table lit by tall, columnar candlesticks. Oversized menus are rolled into glasses. Coffees are served prettily in cups and saucers and pastries on plates of clear pressed glass. The pastry case alongside the espresso bar displays tarts as if they were works of art, complete with labels set off in glittery frames.

# Sunburst Espresso Bar

206 Third Ave. at 18th St. ∼ 674-1702

*Monday to Thursday 7 A.M. to 11 P.M.;*
*Friday and Saturday 7 A.M. to Midnight; Sunday 8 A.M. to 11 P.M.*

WALKING INTO SUNBURST is like entering a fire zone, so intensely brilliant is the ruddy orange-red that cloaks all surfaces and neon-wraps the food-and-drink cases. Extra bursts of color are provided by rays fanning out from wall halogens, as well as by specialty espressos such as the grand royale with orange and lemon syrups. Black blinko/granito counters in the windows are deeper than usual, easier on those who want to take in a crossword puzzle or a chubby scone invigorated with sundried tomatoes and broccoli. P.S. Check out Sunburst's business card; it translates a coffee bean into a hot kiss. Smack!

# Terramare

22 E. 65th St. bet. Fifth and Madison Aves. ∼ 717-5020

*Monday through Friday 8 A.M. to 7:30 P.M.;*
*Saturday 9 A.M. to 7 P.M.; Sunday 10 A.M. to 5 P.M.*

IT'S AS IF A RAY OF SUNSHINE danced in from the Mediterranean to this cheerful little place near the Central Park Zoo. It boasts golden sponge-painted walls and zig-zaggy shelves highlighted in neon-bright green. Faux stone-topped tables can be dragged out to the sidewalk on warm days. Terramare offers a range of mouthwatering desserts which can be savored at leisure, such as a sublimely rich Black Forest cake and a torta della nonna. The clientele here is international, the sort that can simultaneously—and breezily—scan a newspaper and ogle a leg. Just like in *Italia*.

## The 39th Street Cupcake Cafe and Bakery

522 Ninth Ave. at 39th St.  ∼  465-1530
*Monday through Friday 7 A.M. to 7:30 P.M.;*
*Saturday 8 A.M. to 6 P.M.; Sunday 9 A.M. to 5 P.M.*

THE RETRO DECOR and old-time radio crooner music of the Cupcake appears to be a throwback to the '40s. The only thing that pulls you back into the present is the view of one of the ramps into the Lincoln Tunnel, and the parking lot across the street. Views are not what count here, though; it's the cupcakes. Yup, there are cupcakes—lots and lots of them, both traditional yellow and Devil's Food, thickly iced with white or chocolate frosting and topped with icing flower blossoms. All cupcakes, and large flower-festooned celebration cakes, are baked right on the premises. Other treats to offset your Buffalo China mug of coffee (regular or black, nothing fancy here) include trucker-sized slabs of blueberry coffeecake and chunky wedges of the cafe's high-top pies, featured in the Ninth Avenue window.

## Uncommon Grounds

533 Third Ave. bet. 35th and 36th Sts. ∼ 889-5037

*Monday through Wednesday 7 A.M. to 10 P.M.; Thursday 7 A.M. to 11 P.M.;*
*Friday 7 A.M. to Noon; Saturday 8 A.M. to Noon; Sunday 10 A.M. to 10 P.M.*

LIKE SO MANY OF THE COFFEE "INDEPENDENTS," Uncommon Grounds is tiny and elegantly detailed. The logo—a swirly rendition of a cup and saucer with a flourish of steam coiled above, is blazoned on the glass frontage. This logo recurs as a design motif within, where everything is pale yet substantive, rendered in blond wood, stainless steel, and marble. Thick white pine counters are bevel-edged and a stainless-steel filet runs along the blond-painted walls. The tops of the tiny, high tables are incised with stainless steam-swirls; the lowbacked metal stools have surprisingly comfortable blond plyform seats. The white and grey marble barista counter is a mere wedge set diagonally to afford extra space. Cake by the slice, muffins, cookies, sandwiches, and biscotti surf on wavy stainless steel trays.

## Yura & Company

1650 Third Ave. at 92nd St. ∼ 860-8060

*Monday through Saturday 7 A.M. to 11 P.M.; Sunday 8 A.M. to 11 P.M.*

AS OFTEN AS NOT, Yura and partner Paul can be found daily at their roomy and imaginative take-out food market and cafe-restaurant, sampling a new chocolate cake, or cookies warm from the big catering-size kitchen, visibly bustling at the back. This was a bare, supermarket-like corner before the two transformed it into a friendly, affable, countrified place that feels downright neighborly. How it was done: lots of light, a low, duckboard ceiling with upside-down, star-pattern colanders serving as lampshades, painted wainscotting, a creamy floor cheerfully splatter-painted, and tables partnered with green-painted wooden chairs, both new and old. Up front there's a big pine "community table" where you can drink your coffee-to-go, and nibble on an orange-date muffin (Yura's favorite). But there are so many treats to try. Where to begin? Angel food cake with lemon icing, perhaps; or chocolate mini-cupcakes (they star at children's parties on the Upper East Side); "Teddy's cake," dense with apples and nuts; sticky buns, a wonderful lemon curd tart.

## Zido's Coffee and Espresso Bar

294 Third Ave. bet. 22nd and 23rd Sts. ∽ 533-0948
*Monday through Friday 7 A.M. to Midnight;*
*Saturday 8 A.M. to 1 A.M.; Sunday 8 A.M. to Midnight*

A GENIAL NEWCOMER to this neighborhood around the corner from the School of Visual Arts, Zido's imparts a mellow library-like aura. The palette here is comforting and refreshing in its tapestry-toned warmth: soft heather-green walls offset brick, burnished bronze (instead of strident silver) subdues the tin ceiling, there's a luscious burnt-orange counter, and, for a change, highly polished oak floors which add to the overall glow. At the back of the cafe, a cozy lounge area with a deep low banquette and coffee table encourages huddling. Art and photography exhibits rotate through-out. Of the half-dozen loaf cakes offered, the orange yogurt and the lemon poppy stand out. At the front of the cafe, a table displays a selection of beans; customers can measure out—and grind—their own Kenya, Mocha Java, French Roast, or House Blend.

## Zigolini's Famiglia

66 Pearl St. bet. William and Broad Sts. ～ 425-7171
*Monday through Friday 7 A.M. to 7 P.M.*

RIGHT IN THE HEART of the financial district is a full block of ruddy brick houses which remains as a souvenir of Manhattan's seafaring past. Here, where Coenties Alley and Slip meet, you could swear (if you don't look up at the surrounding office towers) you were on Nantucket. Zigolini's Famiglia, steps up from the street, offers an old-style, Italian-style welcome and coffee, either in the front room dominated by a huge wood-faced bar and food cases (and by a bust of Michelangelo's David) or in the back in a chum-my brick-walled room with mirrored arches indented over a quar-tet of cozy booths. Photo blow-ups of amorously inclined couples create a romantic mood, which is reinforced by shimmering chan-deliers. At lunchtime, from 12:30 to 2:30, live jazz provides easy listening, too.

Coffee on
the Run

# Ansonia Espresso Bar

2113 Broadway bet. 72nd and 73rd Sts. ∼ 873-3245

*Daily 7 A.M. to 7 P.M.*

TUCKED INTO THE HEM of the grand old Ansonia apartment building's skirt as it brushes Broadway, this compact venue dressed in smoky mirrors is like a kids' dream of candyland, with its immaculate, militarily aligned ranks of glass candy containers lining the wall behind the counter, their chrome lids twinkling invitingly under the halogen lights. All your childhood favorites are here too, from candy corn to jelly beans of every flavor, chocolate-covered nuts, liquorice allsorts, and gummy worms. At the back, a tiny take-out counter offers Italian and flavored coffees to go or stay; juices, too. Modest seating at the window allows you to peer through the neon signage as you nibble a chocolate-dipped pretzel and inhale espresso.

# Barocco To Go

121 Greenwich Ave. bet. 12th and 13th Sts. ∼ 366-6110

*Monday through Saturday 9 A.M. to 9 P.M.; Sunday 9 A.M. to 7 P.M.*

THE GURGLE FROM A MINIATURE ROCK FOUNTAIN entices passersby into the Greenwich Avenue branch of the restaurant of the same name. Overlooking this alluring windowscape, a rubbed-stainless blade of a counter is a perfect lean-upon spot to sip an espresso and count the leaves remaining on Barocco's intrepid poinsettia plant. A highlight of the impeccably appointed space is the framed group of Polaroids, by Anita Antonini, who also created Barocco To Go's signature postcard. Of the sweet treats featured here, the mouth-filling pecan bars are a standout, as is the marble cake with coconut glaze.

## Breadsoul Cafe

30 Lincoln Plaza/Broadway bet. 62nd and 63rd Sts. ∼ 765-7309
*Monday through Friday 7:30 A.M. to 10 P.M.;*
*Saturday 7:30 A.M. to 11 P.M.; Sunday 7:30 A.M. to 10 P.M.*

THE ORIGINAL OWNER of this minute coffee bar tucked more than a smidgen of style and wit into its tiny (three stools and standing room for two very close friends) interior. The light switch plate on your left as you enter, sports a blue-and-white cup of coffee; above, the bulletin board displays the front page of the day's *Times*—something to eye as you wait in line for your coffee. The country feeling is established with barn flooring and "rafters" which support a pitched wood roof. In a corner of the window a big, blue glass pitcher filled with wild flowers catches the light. A tilted coffee cup and saucer, real metal spoons, and "sugar cubes" of painted wood frame a small mirror. Tender bite-size mini-muffins, made with loving spoonfuls of nuts and cranberries, prove irresistible.

## Brewbar

327 W. 11th St. bet. Greenwich and Washington Sts.  ⌒  807-7384
13 Eighth Ave. at 12th St.  ⌒  243-5297
*Monday through Friday 7 A.M. to 8 P.M.;*
*Saturday 8 A.M. to 8 P.M.; Sunday 9 A.M. to 8 P.M.*

A BRIGHT BLUE FACADE and snappy red umbrella entice Villager and wanderer alike to the way-west 11th Street Brewbar, located a scant block from the glinting waters of the Hudson River. Inside, sunny yellow walls and wedge counters complement the coffee lineup which includes two specials—one called Henry's Blend and another, dear to our Oz-y soul, called Emerald City. The goody baskets offer almond and coconut brownies, almond and chocolate/hazelnut biscotti, pecan fudge bars, lemon and espresso shortbreads, and gingerbread. If it's nice outdoors, you can park yourself and your treats on a bench, or at the single table set out on the sidewalk, and watch the tides roll in, or out, at the end of the street. A few blocks away, on Eighth Avenue, the second Brewbar surveys a far busier scene.

## Brio 2 Go

786 Lexington Ave. at 61st St.  ⌒  980-2300
*Monday through Friday 10 A.M. to 10 P.M.*

BRIO 2 GO is actually located around the corner on 61st Street—it connects with its chic-bistro parent through a common kitchen. You'll catch sight of this impromptu cafe's pretty terra-cotta-pink interior through vivid cantaloupe-painted french doors as you walk toward Park Avenue. The marble cafe table and dainty patina'd cast-iron bench in front appears to be waiting for you to sit down with a cappuccino and Torta di Mele, or morning croissant. Should you prefer, there's another little table and two bistro chairs inside the hallway-sized space, along with a stainless-steel buffet set up with enticing bakery treats, dessert and fashiony foods to go.

## Cafe Bari

529 Broadway at Spring St. ～ 431-4350
*Daily 7 A.M. to 8 P.M.*

THE INDUSTRIAL DEMEANOR of Cafe Bari bespeaks a brisk, efficient approach to dispensing brews. In terms of decor, lite-metal is the order of the day: stainless-steel bar; pretty but proletarian black-and-white mosaic-tiled floors, slim-legged high stools (black, natch) snugly ranked along the bar in the Spring Street window, a couple of high marble-topped tables on the Broadway side. Check out the flavored coffees of the day, or, if you want to remain consistent to Bari's image, go with a hot shot of black.

# Cafe Grand Marnier
1752 Broadway at 56th St. ∼ 581-5130
*Daily 7 A.M. to 10 P.M.*

FRONTING BROADWAY AND 56TH STREET, the two plate-glass walls of the Grand Marnier take in the comings and goings of a Broadway segueing from the high-jinks of Lettermanland into Columbus Circle. Inside, an enormous clock dominates the two-story space with its handful of tables, plus a narrow balcony overlook for those who take time to sip and ignore the inexorable clunk of the minute hand. The complement of bakery goods and cakes includes, naturally, a Grand Marnier.

# Cafe 1*2*3
Two Park Ave. bet. 32nd and 33rd Sts. ∼ 685-7117
*Monday through Thursday 7 A.M. to 9 P.M.; Friday 7 A.M. to 3 P.M.; Sunday 11 A.M. to 8 P.M.*

OWNER ED KAMENITZER says this is the only kosher espresso bar and cafe in the city. It's also one of few places on lower Park where you can find a caffe latte. Cafe 1*2*3's long, narrow space is dominated by a gleaming, dramatic wall crafted entirely of stainless steel. The espresso bar is here, too, right up front where it counts. Some 1950s-style lampshades add a quirky note, and two televisions can be monitored as you wait for your cup of joe. The old-fashioned apple pie à la mode is generous and sweet; the chocolate fudge brownie rich, and the Very Fresh Fruit Cup is what it purports to be.

# Caffe Tosca

260 E. 72nd St. bet. Second and Third Aves. ～ 744-4155
*Daily 7:30 A.M. to 7 P.M.*

IF THE DOOR IS OPEN AS YOU PASS, you may indeed hear
Puccini's *Tosca* (in any one of the owner's six recordings). Opera-
related images hang on the walls: a portrait of Verdi, posters, a cut-
away view of the Met showing a production in process. Black tubular bar chairs edge up to faux-granite counters and there are two
cafe-height tables for the perching crowd. Eight kinds of coffees are
sold as bean or brew; for sweets, try the fruit smoothies, homemade
lemon drop gems or blueberry crumb muffins, and "feather" cake.

# Chelsea's Espresso Bar

210 Seventh Ave. at 22nd St. ～ 206-8033
58 Third Ave. bet. 10th and 11th Sts. ～ 777-2463
*Monday through Thursday 8 A.M. to 11 P.M.; Friday 8 A.M. to Midnight;*
*Saturday 8:30 A.M. to Midnight; Sunday 9 A.M. to 11 P.M.*

"SIT DOWN WITH US and have a cappuccino, latte, or cafe au
lait—hot or (iced) cold," requests the chalkboard at the cheerful
West Side branch of this espresso bar. Pull up a blue-cushioned
stool to the copper counter in the south-facing window; if it's too
sunny, blue acrylic shades can be pulled down to temper the glare.
Shelves display over three-dozen varieties of beans, including
unroasted greens, and several sleek coffee machines by manufactur-
ers DeLonghi and Bosch. *The Wizard of Oz* gang and the Lone

Ranger and his trusty sidekick Tonto cast their collective eye upon the denizens of the bar; we're not sure what their coffee connection is—maybe they're just reinforcing the notion of comraderie. The same goes for the East Side branch, which has a congenially appointed back area plumped with a couple of loveseats and cozy chairs. This venue also offers a ten percent discount to students during the school year when they show their college I.D.

## Coffeearts Espresso Bar

124 Fulton St. bet. Nassau and Dutch Sts. ~ 227-5857
*Monday through Friday 6 A.M. to 6 P.M.*

LOCATED JUST OFF THE NASSAU STREET pedestrian mall in the No-Man's land that joins City Hall and the financial district, Coffeearts is sandwiched between an electronics shop and a watch/perfume shop on a rather seedy-looking discount block of Fulton Street near the South Street Seaport. Coffeearts itself, though, is distinctly upmarket and handsome, with an undulating wooden espresso/pastry bar embellished with a silvery wave-shaped toeplate. A green marble counter in one window and wooden "splinter" in the other are perfect perch-points to grab a cup of espresso and observe the action in the street.

## Coffee Cherries

13 E. 4th St. bet. Broadway and Lafayette St. ～ 475-8551
*Monday through Friday 8 A.M. to 8 P.M.;*
*Saturday and Sunday 10 A.M. to 7 P.M.*

THIS SPARTAN WHITE-AND-BLACK LOFT BAR near Astor Place
serves up its joe-to-go in a straightforward, utilitarian atmosphere.
As an accompaniment to your coffee, try one of Cherries' tempting
"coffee master" sweets. One's an incredibly chewy chocolate truffle
brownie. Included in over a dozen muffins is a fat-free, low-choles-
terol one called "Blue Angel." Hena Estate-Grown beans are sold
along one wall; check out the one they call "Rockslide," which is
roasted with chocolate. Yum. Once you've attained the zap you
desire, mosey across the street to prolong your buzz at Tower
Records—where, by the time you read this, there'll probably be a
coffee bar, too.

## The Coffee Sack, Inc.

343 W. 14th St. bet. Eighth and Ninth Aves. ～ 647-0444
*Monday through Friday 7:30 A.M. to 6 P.M.; Saturday 11 A.M. to 6 P.M.*

BEFORE THE ARRIVAL OF THIS SHOP in the rawboned ware-
house-and-trucking district near the Hudson River and West Side
Highway, there was literally nowhere in the area to go for a cup of
coffee, or beans. The Coffee Sack is neither trendy nor arty,
just a bare-essentials wood-and-brick sort of place. Except
for a huge neon coffee cup behind the counter, the shop is virtually

unadorned. There are twenty kinds of beans to purchase by the pound. Next to the counter are two kinds of yummies: melt-in-your-coffee mocha "spoons" and chocolate-covered mint double-dip sticks. There's also a bowl of Coffee Sack-embossed wooden nickels; we keep ours on hand for emergencies. Country and western music is supplied by a boombox.

## Condotti

237 E. 53rd St. bet. Second and Third Aves. ∽ 688-6886
*Monday through Friday 8 A.M. to 5:30 P.M.; Saturday 10 A.M. to 4 P.M.*

SQUEEZED INTO THE FRONT PARLOR of a now slightly raffish brownstone, Condotti's palazzo-prego mood is established by sunnily distressed walls and four carved rococo wood high chairs upholstered in green pinstripe velvet. A playful trompe l'oeil ceiling reveals a monkey frisking against a blue sky. Behind the minute counter with its cookies and pastries, asymmetrically sliced copper swingdoors hide a full kitchen. Espresso comes in a doll-sized china "coffee can" whose metal handle is no bigger than a pinkie ring. Home-baked highlights: folded points of fruit-dabbed shortbread cookies that are sweet, buttery mouthfuls, as are espresso-and-ricotta muffins.

# Corrado Cafe and Espresso Bar

1013 Third Ave. at 60th St. ～ 753-5100

*Monday 7 A.M. to 9 P.M.; Tuesday, Wednesday, and Thursday 7 A.M. to 9 P.M.;*
*Friday 7 A.M. to Midnight; Saturday 8 A.M. to Midnight; Sunday 9 A.M. to 9 P.M.*

HANDILY LOCATED NEAR BLOOMINGDALE'S and close to movie theaters and interior-design buildings, the Corrado Cafe knows who its clientele is: people who need to punctuate a flick or shopping outing with a caffeine fix. Coffee and sweets are served to the left of the entrance in the Espresso Bar, offering an array of creamy cakes and gateaux by the slice, cookies, wrapped-chocolate bonbons by the piece, and muffins galore—still plentiful and fresh late in the day—plus ice creams. The surroundings are blondish and '50s-ish, with oak counters and high tables. On a sunny spring day, head out through the back door to seat yourself in the public Savoy Plaza, where you can bask in the pale rays and admire the trees.

# Davis & Webb

1592B Third Ave at 89th St. ～ 369-7198

*Daily 8 A.M. to 7 P.M.*

MESSRS. DAVIS & WEBB have created a cozy nook here on Third Avenue. To say there's seating, though, is a bit of a stretch under the usual crowd conditions; still, you might get a shot at the squashy windowseat. Otherwise, it's standing room only. Headshots of theatrical wanna-bes are pinned up on the wall; your chance to spot tomorrow's talent on the way up. D&W sells around one hundred blends—sixty regular and about forty decaf, roasted to Sam Webb's personal specifications. French Roast "gets taken back to Paris;" Espresso and Guatemala Viennese are also hot. Baked goods are from the Columbus Bakery.

## Espresso Bar, The Original

82 Christopher St. bet. Seventh Ave. and Bleecker St. ~ 627-3870
*Monday through Friday 7 A.M. to Midnight;*
*Saturday and Sunday 8 A.M. to 3 A.M.*

THIS HIGH-CEILINGED, narrow wedge of a space off "Stonewall Square" is hip with gays, as well it should be in this location. Open only for a couple of years, the bar looks and feels right at home—as if it had been part of the scene far longer. There's a room-long counter with so many stools it could seat a chorus line. Across the way, cases and tiered stands display an impressive array of sweets in portions ample enough to share. Lemon, pumpkin, and espresso "bars" are huge, as is a brownie so dense and rich you'd swear you'd died and gone to heaven. The buzz is always on; in fact, the barista says the bar will stay open all night long on weekends during the spring and summer if there's a soul left in the place after 3 A.M.

## Espresso Madison

33 E. 68th St. bet. Madison and Park Aves. ~ 988-7444
*Monday through Saturday 8 A.M. to 6:30 P.M.*

MY, THIS IS A POSH BLOCK, lined with embassy-style townhous-
es, and anchored at the corner of Park by the Americas Society.
Admire the copper roofs of Numbers 39 and 41, skim past the
exquisite childrens' clothing store, and eccola!, you're in front of
Espresso Madison. Prepare to be very Euro-chic as you step down
into the place, vibrant with melodic jazz. The well-dressed denizens
will give you a razor-quick once-over before returning to their
caffe. Like a jewel box of mahogany and mirror, punctuated with
Fornasetti accessories, low-ceilinged Espresso Madison resounds to
banter in several languages. Two low stools snuggle up to the
counter/sill at an open window; two folding chairs center on a wire
spool table. For the rest, everyone stands Italian-style, elbow-to-
elbow at the bar, where wine and champagne are served along with
authentico Lavazza caffe.

## Fluffy's Cafe & Bakery

855 Seventh Ave. bet. 54th and 55th Sts. ~ 247-0234
*Daily 7 A.M. to 10 P.M.*

TWENTY YEARS AGO, Fluffy's opened to serve up their name-
brand doughnuts—and donuts, telegraphically updated—are still
the way to go here. Trendier decor details include a faux clouded-
sky ceiling, sponge-daubed walls, and tall ruddy-marble topped

tables for noshing on a donut-to-stay. Regular donuts—over twenty types of deliciously portly "O"s—range from honey-dipped glazed to vanilla frosted to sugar-raised to chocolate sprinkled. All can be purchased individually, or by the half-dozen or dozen. If donuts don't suit you, baklava, strudel, fresh fruit torte, and a wide assortment of cakes tempt from the pastry case.

## Helena's

694 Columbus Ave. at 94th St. ~ 864-7340
*Monday through Saturday 10 A.M. to 5 P.M.*

THERE IS IN FACT A HELENA, and she does work the counter sometimes. The space itself, well-lit by lights that are set in a track on the red ceiling, is paved in black and white tile, which goes nicely with the white walls and the counters. A long counter in a false-stone pattern bears a large selection of baked goods and coffees and extends into the window to serve as a kind of centerpiece of foodstuffs. A small recessed counter to the right of the door boasts three stools, the total number Helena's can seat. A good-sized cup of coffee and a behemoth of a muffin are an affordable treat.

## J.P.'s French Bakery

54 W. 55th St. bet. Fifth and Sixth Aves. ～ 765-7575
*Monday through Friday 7 A.M. to 7 P.M.;*
*Saturday 8 A.M. to 6 P.M.; Sunday 8 A.M. to 5 P.M.*

BILLING ITSELF AS "LA MAISON DU CROISSANT," J.P.'s actually
presents a far greater galaxy of baked goods and sweet treats, from
sixty-four breads, muffins, and scones—at last count—to myriad
cookies, pastries, and tarts. White-tiled walls, hanging baskets and
dried flowers, vintage photos framed in burgundy mats, and a couple of high wooden counters with farm stools pulled up to them
establish the French country theme here. At the back of the shop, a
tiny, woodsy hideaway alcove sheathed with sides of wine cases harbors a trio of tables and folding chairs; it's a perfect place to take a
cafe au lait and pastry "to stay."

## JW Espresso Bar

1709 Second Ave. bet. 88th and 89th Sts. ～ 427-4008
*Monday through Saturday 7 A.M. to 9 P.M.; Sunday 9 A.M. to 7 P.M.*

THE NICE THING about independent coffee bars is their individual personalities, like JW's. Arrive early enough in the A.M. and you
may see the owner cleaning the windows while keeping an eye on a
customer's dogs tied up outside. Since JW's is right by the bus stop
you can dash in for caffe—or sit for a moment or two at one of
two sidewalk tables, among planters of flowers, until your order
arrives. The interior's exposed brick walls and high tin ceiling

speak of brownstone origins; a couple of large antique-like mirrors allow you to gaze at yourself and others while you nibble a muffin from a flowered plate or sip coffee from a real china cup, hooray! Of the eight plain and flavored coffees offered daily, try the "Full City" blend, a dark punch of caffeine.

## Madison Avenue's Honest Baker

1006 Madison Ave. bet. 77th and 78th Sts. ∼ 717-1144
*Monday through Friday 7 A.M. to 9:30 P.M.;*
*Saturday and Sunday 9 A.M. to 7 P.M.*

AS THE ARCHITECTURALLY ELEGANT INTERIOR took shape, locals figured on an expensive boutique. But Elena Castaneda just wanted to create the perfect setting for her worldly bakery and low-fat treats whose computer-analyzed nutritional values, fat, and calorie costs are stated on labels next to the mouth-wateringly decorative foods. But still, tastebuds may go into spin as you enter: what to eat, and what not? Clue: the "cake" in the window is a light fixture. Exquisite confections in the cherry wood cabinet are faux—dried flowers, grass and leaves, alas. Real enough: blueberry crumb cake (one slice, 158 grams; 390 calories; fat, 40 calories), palmiers, oatmeal cookies, and apple muffin tops sprinkled with sunflower seeds. Love object: delicate tarte tatin. Coffee: plenty of it.

## The Muffins Shop

222 Columbus Ave. bet. 70th and 71st Sts. ∼ 875-1173

*Daily 7 A.M. to 7 P.M.*

THERE'S SMALL, and then there's smaller. In some way, The Muffins Shop brings to mind a walk-in baker's oven—the kind with an arched ceiling. Upon entering the shop, notice the elements of the hemisphere mirror that resemble plane elevations of muffin tops; and how the white walls, the wooden arch motif behind the counter, and the black and white tile floor all evoke the kind of boulangerie you'd find in a French village. The Muffins Shop's wares are baked by the Connecticut Muffin Company; try the dense five-grain muffins, which will satisfy your craving for something that's sweet, but healthful. The American coffee comes from Dallis Brothers of Ozone Park; the Italian coffee is supplied by Moca d'Oro, a long-established Brooklyn coffee merchant.

## Neuman & Bogdonoff

1385 Third Ave. bet. 78th and 79th St. ∼ 861-0303

*Monday through Friday 6:30 A.M. to 8:30 P.M.;*
*Saturday 7 A.M. to 7:30 P.M.; Sunday 8 A.M. to 6:30 P.M.*

IT'S SUNDAY MORNING, and you've just done your run. For once you're early, the sun shines, the park sparkles, and you feel great . . . all you need is a breakfast cup of good Italian coffee and a little reward for getting out there—say, a babka muffin, or a savory scone. And here is Neuman & Bogdonoff, kindly open. Plop yourself down at one of two tables surrounded by counters devoted to glorious foods, exotic cans of this and that, continental edibles, Manhattan's usual cornucopia of gourmet fancies. As you await your coffee—flavor of the day, or cafe au lait, perhaps—cast your eye on the food possibilities to take home for later. Friends coming for lunch? You can pick it all up here.

## Newsbar

366 W. Broadway at Broome St.  ∼  343-0053
*Monday to Friday 8 A.M. to 7 P.M.;*
*Saturday and Sunday 9 A.M. to 7 P.M.*
107 University Pl. bet. 11th and 12th Sts.  ∼  260-4192
*Monday through Friday 7 A.M. to Midnight;*
*Saturday and Sunday 7 A.M. to 1 A.M.*
2 W. 19th St. bet. Fifth and Sixth Aves.  ∼  255-3996
*Daily 6 A.M. to 8 P.M.*
969 Third Ave. bet. 56th and 57th Sts.  ∼  319-0830
*Monday through Friday 8 A.M. to 9 P.M.;*
*Saturday and Sunday 9 A.M. to 7 P.M.*

NEWSBAR DELIVERS A TRIPLE ZAP: Headline news on overhead TVs; hundreds of foreign and domestic journals, periodicals, and newspapers—plus, of course, multiple takes on espresso. The West Broadway venue is sliced across the corner outside on a diagonal and swing-out galvanized steel racks—for mags ranging from *Eye* to *Elle*—are tethered by guy-wires and flagged for the info-hungry: "STAND to browse"; "SIT DOWN pay up." Perch-at tables provide three stools on casters, which can be rolled to or away depending upon one's penchant for aloofness. Of the espressos, three stand out: "Latte de Soia," with soy milk, "Skinny," a no-fat latte, and "No Fun," decaf with no-fat latte.

## The Nickel Cup

247 E. 57th St. bet. Second and Third Aves. ~ 355-6653
*Monday through Friday 6 A.M. to 10 P.M.;*
*Saturday 8 A.M. to 11 P.M.; Sunday 8 A.M. to 10 P.M.*

WALK EAST ON 57TH STREET and there's the Nickel Cup, next to a chandelier and lighting store. The spare, white painted interior is dramatized by murals of the city—one a '70s-style black-and-silver version of the skyline; the other a sepia-and-cream "drawing" evoking a city of the past. Fixtures are constructed in dark wood. Six dark green marble tables lined up along one wall lead the eye toward—guess what? A tiny patio out back, with three more tables and potted geraniums sunning themselves on a wrought iron and marble shelf. To go: sixteen varieties of White House coffees, the beans stored in natural wood "barrels."

## Positively 99

2621 Broadway at 99th St. ~ 666-0099
*Monday through Friday 7 A.M. to 9 P.M.;*
*Saturday 7:30 A.M. to 8 P.M.; Sunday 7:30 A.M. to 6 P.M.*

THE ONLY COFFEE PLACE FOR BLOCKS, pocket-sized Positively 99 is located opposite the decaying Metro Cinema (check out the elegant art deco relief soaring above the moviehouse's entrance). All the coffee drinks you seek can be found on the "Coffee Break" list on the wall. A pink laminate counter offers cinnamon rolls, fruit and berry muffins, and the like; there's also a sandwich-making section. Black high-tech sales racks tucked around a small cold-drinks unit offer Bread Alone's hearty offerings and an edited selection of gourmet items. Eight bar chairs are planted at a polished dark steel counter if you wish to ingest on the spot.

## Re-Union

301 W. 57th St. bet. Eighth and Ninth Aves. ~ 586-4152
*Monday through Friday 6 A.M. to 8:30 P.M.;*
*Saturday 7 A.M. to 8:30 P.M.; Sunday 7 A.M. to 6:30 P.M.*

NOTCHED INTO A HIGH-RISE just off the cusp of Columbus Circle, this minuscule coffee bar is a welcome amenity at the north end of Eighth Avenue. Pale citrus walls accented with beveled-board wainscot and mahogany-toned molding and counter—and four comfortable, matching bar chairs—afford a tranquil, country-like demeanor to the place. The sipping stand-out here is a short shot of espresso daubed with a dollop of panna or whipped cream. Re-Union's sour cream coffee upside-down minibundt is tasty, as is the pistacio flat, a sharp tangy cookie shaped much like a biscotto.

## Rimsky-Korsakoffee Espresso Bar

1179 Second Ave. bet. 62nd and 63rd Sts.
*Monday through Saturday 8 A.M. to 8 P.M*

AT A GLANCE you'll discern the whimsical and witty spirit that sets this coffee bar apart. Above the awning, painted coffee cups dance with a musical note; the window displays a painted profile of Rimsky-Korsakov himself (his music can be heard indoors). On the sidewalk, a little wooden bench sports jaunty cup and saucer cut-outs. The menu is printed on sheet music; on the back wall is a montage of musical play—a violin, a bow, an opera mask. Sweet potato, cherry and banana loaves, Norwegian marzipan cake, "Mormor's Sjokoladekake," and the like are nestled in baskets tucked in with brilliant plaid napkins. Coffee drinks include Almond Rocha Mocha, espresso combined with chocolate and almond and hazelnut flavorings and steamed milk topped with whipped cream. European and Hamptons' newspapers on a wall rack complete the menu of distinctive small pleasures.

# The Royale Pastry Shop

237 W. 72nd St. bet. Broadway and West End Ave. ～ 874-5642
*Monday through Thursday 6 A.M. to 8 P.M.; Friday 6 A.M. to sundown.;*
*Sunday 7 A.M. to 7 P.M. Closed July, all Jewish holidays, Saturdays*

THE ROYALE PASTRY SHOP decor is WWII West Side utilitarian—old fashioned laminate, white tiles, non-matching stainless steel refrigeration cases—one of which, laboring enthusiastically in its mission to chill the perishable cream cakes, sounds like a Pratt-Whitney engine just before take-off. But the charm of the place transcends all, embodied in the old world courtesy of the staff and the wonderful sweets. Hamantashen, rugeleh, potatonicks, and masterful breads (the corn rye has sustained generations of West Siders) sell out before you can say "enjoy." There are big Swiss rolls, humongous eclairs with oodles of chocolate icing, crumbly muffins, layer cakes, danish, strudel, pies, Russian coffee cake, and cookies lying in heaps on numbered trays (fun for kids to ask for four of number five, seven of number nine, etc). Help yourself to a cup of American joe from the Bunn unit on the right in the back of the store, jockey for one of the six red vinyl chairback stools, and read the community and event posters from the local temples as you munch.

## Seattle Coffee Roasters

150 Fifth Ave. bet. 18th and 19th Sts. ~ 675-9700
*Monday through Thursday 7 A.M. to 9 P.M.;*
*Friday and Saturday 7 A.M. to Midnight; Sunday 7 A.M. to 8 P.M.*
188 Columbus Ave. bet. 68th and 69th Sts. ~ 877-6699
*Monday through Thursday 7 A.M. to 11 P.M.; Friday 7 A.M. to 1 A.M.;*
*Saturday 8 A.M. to 1 A.M.; Sunday 8 A.M. to Midnight*

ANSEL ADAMS WOULD BE PROUD of this coffee bar in the Photographers' District, subscribing as it does to a high-contrast black and white palette—with tone-corrected gray "zones" between. As might be expected, the decor includes huge blow-ups suspended in minimalist black frames (of course). The skinny granite perch-at counters zipping along the wall opposite the espresso bar are accented with clever Plexiglas tubes filled with beans. To off-set the hard-edged and high-tech, cacti wrapped in kraft paper and tied with twine are spotted about. Sixteen tables, in tidy T-square grid formation, serve the back portion of the cafe. Music pulses; the Belgian chocolate brownie beckons; the cappuccino foams on cue. It could be a shoot.

## Sticky Fingers Bake Shop

131 Ave. A bet. St. Mark's Pl. and 9th St. ~ 614-0560
*Daily 7 A.M. to 8 P.M.*

THIS SLICE OF A BAKERY across from the children's playground in Tompkins Square Park is appropriately adorned with the artwork of the owners' small daughter. The winsome touch of the child is everywhere in evidence here. Signs on the baked goodies which may accompany an espresso and cappuccino to go, for example, are handwritten. Sweets are almost too overwhelming in their extravagance: Marble brownies and chocolate chip cookies are absolutely humongous. Brownies and Oreo brownies are extolled, rightly, as "massive and dense." If the sheer generosity of their size overtakes you, pleat yourself into a child's chair and consume your goodie and java on the spot. Then work it off on the swingset across the street.

# World Cup Cafe & Bakery

956 Lexington Ave. bet. 70th and 71st Sts.  ∼  717-6888
*Monday through Friday 7:30 A.M. to 8 P.M.;*
*Saturday 9 A.M. to 6 P.M.*

JUST TWO BLOCKS NORTH of Hunter College and on the beeline into the 68th Street IRT, the diminutive World Cup—only 6' x 14'—is one of those holes in the wall that confer upon this city its particular pulse and elan. Sponge-painted walls superimposed with a wainscoted dado and a window seat plumped with three cushions lend World Cup an air of the country. For folks who want to perch for a spell, there's *The Observer, Money, Time, Vanity Fair, Cosmo,* and *Self*. Over a dozen varieties of muffin are identified by the appropriate fruit, veg slice, berry, or chip (as in chocolate) embedded in their puffed-up crowns. World Cup also offers nine varieties of bean by the pound.

# Old-time Coffeehouses & Pasticcerias

# Bleecker Street Pastry & Cafe

245 Bleecker St. bet. Leroy and Cornelia Sts.  ~  242-4959

*Monday through Thursday 7:30 A.M. to 10 P.M.;*
*Friday and Saturday 7:30 A.M. to Midnight; Sunday 8 A.M. to 10 P.M.*

DEEP MAHOGANY-TONED WALLS with mirrored insets and softly whirring ceiling fans create an ambiance of genteel calm on this otherwise touristy stretch of Bleecker Street. Besides the traditional Italian pastries, there's a treat unique to this shop: a tantalizing sunflower cake with chocolate sprinkle "seeds." If you choose to stay and sample cannoli or one of the other delectables, the espresso bar is at the far end of the shop.

# Cafe Borgia

185 Bleecker St. at MacDougal St.  ~  674-9589

*Monday through Friday 10:30 A.M. to 3 A.M.;*
*Saturday and Sunday 10:30 A.M. to 5 A.M.*

A FLAKING MURAL INSPIRED BY BOTTICELLI and other masters of the Italian Renaissance adorns one wall of this old-timer on the Bleecker/MacDougal Four Corners (others harbor the Carpo, the MacDougal, and Le Figaro). Upgrading a time-burnished image is not an issue here. The floor is black linoleum, the tables are marble-topped, the chairs, charming swirled iron—and the pastries, including cappuccino mousse cake, basic and tasty. The point is to hang out and converse; there's no entertainment except what you bring to the party.

# Cafe Borgia II

161 Prince St. bet. Thompson St. and W. Broadway ∼ 677-1850
*Sunday through Thursday 10 A.M. to Midnight;*
*Friday and Saturday 10 A.M. to 2 A.M.*

POLISHED KNOTTY-PINE AND BRICK WALLS, wood-like laminate tables, and metal cafe chairs set the plainspoken tone here, one that's easy on the eyes and ears if you want, quite simply, to step off the boulevard that is West Broadway and sip in quiet surroundings. Sweets are plainspoken, too: check out the strawberry-peach, chocolate mousse, and blueberry crumb cakes. Three tables offer sidewalk sun time.

# Caffe Biondo

141 Mulberry St. bet. Grand and Houston Sts. ∼ 226-9285
*Sunday through Thursday Noon to 1 A.M.;*
*Friday and Saturday Noon to 2 A.M.*

A HARMONIOUS MIX OF TEXTURES defines this friendly coffee-and-cake stop along Mulberry Street: a thickly trowelled stucco wall behind the long coffee/pastry bar balances the brick wall opposite and a mirrored one at the back of the narrow space. The cake lineup is impressive and includes a rainbow cake in Italian flag hues, a dense, flourless chocolate hazelnut cream torte, a chocolate walnut torte, and an apple cheesecake.

# Caffe Dante

81 MacDougal Street bet. W. Houston and Bleecker Sts. ∼
982-5275
*Daily 10 A.M. to 2 A.M.*

IN BUSINESS FOR NINETY YEARS, Caffe Dante has been one of
the regulars on Greenwich Village's coffeehouse beat. Lighter and
airier in atmosphere than most, this old-world cafe is adorned with
gigantic photomurals of Dante's hometown, Firenze; the poet and
his beloved Beatrice are pictured, too, at the back. The pastry case
is filled with typical Italian delicacies such as toscanella puff pastry
and a torta della nonna.

# Caffe Reggio

119 Macdougal St. bet. W. 3rd and W. 4th Sts. ∼ 475-9557
*Monday to Thursday and Sunday 9 A.M. to 2 A.M.;*
*Friday and Saturday 9 A.M. to 4 A.M.*

AND THE BEAT(NIK) GOES ON. Artfully blending Village funk
with neighborly brio, the dim, coffee-hued Caffe Reggio, "home of
the original cappuccino in the Village," had been in operation for
decades before the influx of the bohemian set. Nothing, in fact, has
shaken Caffe Reggio's resolve to battle the "duel for the best coffee
in the world." Tourists love the hype (and the orange-banded cof-
feeware to purchase as souvenirs), as do the locals—some with kids
in tow. Opera music curls into the gloom; conversation steams the
windows dressed with ancient velvet draperies. Pride of place has

been given a glistening espresso machine dating from 1902. Eighty works of art hang from the moody walls; check out the vast canvas tagged "school of Caravaggio" and the portrait of Cesare Borgia over a bench bearing the crest of the Medici.

## Caffe Roma

385 Broome St. at Mulberry St. ～ 226-8413
518 Washington St., Hoboken, NJ ～ 201-792-3302
*Daily 8 A.M. to Midnight*

WITH ITS DEEP HUNTER-GREEN WALLS, flooring of black-and-white mosaic tile, and tin ceiling, Caffe Roma looks as if it has been rooted to this corner of Little Italy for ages—as indeed it has. Regulars hunch around tables in the window—or toss back their stand-up espresso fix en route to Big Business Deals elsewhere. On Sundays, entire families assemble after Mass for a treat. The pastry cases highlight Italian specialties, including cannolis both plain and chocolate cloaked. As a concession to the tourist crowd that frequents the neighborhood, the cafe sells mugs emblazoned with its logo, beans in six roasts by the pound, and biscotti by the bag. For those who make a daily commute from the other side of the Hudson, there's a sister cafe in Hoboken.

# Ferrara Pasticceria and Espresso Bar

195 Grand St. bet. Mulberry and Mott Sts.  ∼  226-6150

*Daily 8 A.M. to Midnight*

IN BUSINESS SINCE 1892, Ferrara's is a local landmark for pastries and espresso, not only for denizens of Little Italy, but also for the jury duty crowd, and those who dare take the plunge south of Canal. The vast pastry cases and brass espresso bar gleam, as do the mirrors which line the walls. The over three-dozen pastry choices include the expected cannolis and biscotti, as well as babas—rum, ricotta, and cream. A chocolate-covered coconut bombe (for you and yours) stands out, as does the Dadi, a checkerboard of chocolate cake, buttercream, and fudge.

# La Lanterna di Vittorio

129 MacDougal St. bet. 3rd and 4th Sts.  ∼  529-5945

*Sunday through Thursday 10 A.M. to 3 A.M.;*
*Friday and Saturday 10 A.M. to 4 A.M.*

OWNER/HOST VITTORIO ANTONINI can be found taking a sip of his own strong brew near one of the fireplaces in his atmospheric, brick-walled, self-styled "fireside cafe." Windowed front and back, La Lanterna simultaneously eyes the bustle of MacDougal and the tranquility of a garden at the rear. The selection of beverages includes not only the requisite espresso and cappuccino, but also two cocoas, one served up—to children's delight—with marshmallow. Dozens of pastries and many classic Italian sweets are offered.

# Le Figaro Cafe
184 Bleecker St. at MacDougal St. ～ 677-1100
*Sunday through Thursday 11 A.M. to 2 A.M.;*
*Friday and Saturday 10 A.M. to 4 A.M.*

GREENWICH VILLAGE'S LE FIGARO, a den of nooks papered in old French "journaux" fenced in by mocha wrought iron balustrades and lit by huge art nouveau globe lights, is one of the old-time coffeehouses most often nostalgically exhumed by followers of the Beat Generation. The cafe action is along Bleecker Street, a perfect vantage point to check on the tour buses that vrroom by. Coffees with liqueurs and fresh whipped cream are a specialty here: the "Pucci" is laced with Amaretto and rum; the "Pousse," with creme de menthe and brandy. Inside, ogle the raspberry blackout cake, banana cream tart and apple-brown betty in the pastry case. Mondays through Thursdays jazz pumps from 8 to 11:30 P.M.; there's a jazz brunch on Sundays from 1 to 4:30 P.M. and bellydancing on Sunday nights at 9.

# The Peacock Cafe
24 Greenwich Ave. bet. 6th and 7th Sts. ～ 242-9395
*Daily 1 P.M. to 1 A.M.*

AS ARTURO, owner of the Peacock recounts, thirty-five years ago when he came to New York from his native Florence, there were over forty European-style coffeehouses in Greenwich Village. Today, only a handful remain. The name, Peacock, derives from one of the first partners, a barber, in acknowledgment of his countrymen's penchant for a "bella figura." At the Peacock, a vaguely Renaissance aura pervades. Close by the coffee bar, a large portrait of Cosimo de Medici peers benignly over the regulars, some of whom, Arturo asserts, drop in two or three times a day for a quick espresso. One regular, poet Harry Ellison, holds a casual Poet's Circle here Tuesday and Thursday evenings for $4.

## Veniero's Pasticceria & Cafe

342 E. 11 St. bet. First and Second Aves. ∼ 674-7264
*Sunday through Thursday 8 A.M. to Midnight;*
*Friday and Saturday 8 A.M. to 1 A.M.*

ONE HUNDRED YEARS have not diminished Veniero's take-a-check popularity. Enthusiasm continues unabated for their dozens of cakes and pastries. Classics here include torta di mondella, an almond pastry filled with apricot jam, and "Windmill," a chocolate cake filled with chocolate whipped-cream and topped with bitter-sweet chocolate. Veniero's favorite? A mocha espresso cake. Next door is Veniero's equally busy cafe, a narrow marble-and-mirror clad space lit through a huge stained-glass panel set into a bronzed ceiling. Veniero's attracts a convivial crowd. Students hunch over double espressos; aging aunties coo to each other over sweet treats; artists drop in between brushstrokes, babies are weaned on a finger damped with steamed milk. There's something for everyone at Veniero's.

# Franchises
# & Chains

# Chock Full o' Nuts

*Monday through Friday 6:30 A.M. to 6 P.M., Saturday 6:30 A.M. to 5 P.M.*
For branches, call: 754-9600

THE HEAVENLY COFFEE IS BACK! A sprightly yellow-and-black Checker Cab (remember them, too?) logo-strip zips across the cafe's menu; golden oldies issue from the sound system; and blow-up photos of vintage storefronts and stop-bys (including a mobile Chock Full that resembles a house on wheels) all remind us of when a cream-cheese-on-raisin and coffee set us back fifty cents. Well, those days are long past, but the memory lingers on. Stylish now, the cafes are floored in mottled gray quarry tile; tables are seriously functional downtown black; and chairs are modeled from lean planks of henna-toned wood. The cafe offers a rotating selection of varietal and flavored coffees. The Heavenly Bakery roundup includes two pound cakes and soft cookies, one a reduced-fat oatmeal.

# Cooper's Coffee Bars

*Daily 7 A.M. to 8 P.M.*
For branches, call: 496-0100

COOPER'S COFFEE BARS offer a spare setting, composed of yellow flat–painted walls, mahogany counters, and rough–hewn slate, and silvery/stainless-steel elements: the result is a cool, masculine-style interior, and indeed these bars seem to be places where guys hang out—to read, to shoot the breeze, to relax with an espresso between appointments. Characterful baristas dream up the daily quiz found at each branch (prize winners get a free latte). Cooper's roasts green beans every Monday for Tuesday delivery: an all-Arabica regular roast which includes African, Hawaiian, and Central American varieties, a dark roast, a decaf, and hazelnut. Best foodie picks: the savory seven-grain bagels from Cooper's Bagelry and the dried fruit and berry scones.

## Dalton Coffee Ltd. Espresso Cafe

*Daily 7:30 A.M. to 11 P.M.*
For branches, call: 674-8776

ALL DALTONS OCCUPY SOPHISTICATED, all-white spaces trimmed in black. In each a television monitor is soundlessly plugged into CNN or New York's Channel One and jazz or classical music hums softly in the background. A selection of newspapers is available for those who want to check out the lead stories in print. Dalton's calls its roasts Full City, High-Roast, and New York Original. Decafs are dubbed "relaxers"—the one with no-fat milk, a "skinny relaxer."

# New World Coffee

*Monday through Thursday 7 A.M. to 7 P.M.; Friday and Saturday 7 A.M.
to 10 P.M.; Sunday 8 A.M. to 9 P.M. Business-area stores are open Monday
through Friday only and hours vary.*
For branches, call: 343-0552

THE TWENTY OR SO New World Coffee Bars share a similarly
upscale ambiance. The characteristic hand-painted faux effects that
visually texturize one wall, usually behind a white marble counter,
were created by a Vermont artist. Mahogany chairs and tables lend
warmth to the minimalist decor. New World sells four bean blends
and a decaf; no flavored coffees are offered. The popular house blend
is composed of Costa Rican, Sumatran, Kenya AA and Ethiopian coffees. Sweet treats, like the clientele, tend to be on the worldly side.
Cakes include a chocolate Grand Marnier and a lighter-than-air angel
food. Biscotti flavors include chocolate chip espresso.

# New York Coffee Station

One World Trade Center ∼ 488-8717
30 Rockefeller Plaza bet. 48th and 49th Sts. ∼ 582-5139
1221 Sixth Ave. bet. 46th and 47th Sts. ∼ 869-7382
150 E. 52 St. bet. Lexington and Third Aves. ∼ 838-6442
*Monday through Friday 7 A.M. to 6 P.M.*

ONE LEVEL UNDER THE GENERAL-ELECTRIC BUILDING behind Rockefeller Center's skating rink, the art decoesque Coffee Station, formerly known as the Daily Caffe, adroitly juggles joes-to-go for the denizens of 30 Rock—as does its nearby sister two levels underground in the McGraw-Hill Building on Sixth Avenue. The cafe on 52nd Street has a more expansive menu, i.e., soups and sandwiches to go, as well as some seating. A new branch, a snazzy riveted green bar accented in red, stands in an easy pass-by position in the concourse connecting the Twin Towers and is open on the weekend. New branches are due to open soon at One Penn Plaza and in the Empire State Building. Check out our favorite blend, called Dancing Goats, after the legendary frolicking creature who discovered the stimulating bean.

# Oren's Daily Roast

*Monday through Friday 7 A.M. to 7 P.M.; Saturday 10 A.M. to 6 P.M.*
For branches, call: 348-5400

OREN'S HAS PATENTED A LAID–BACK, friendly style, yet each branch has its own design personality—plus a stand–out selection of coffee paraphernalia. The owner roasts and delivers beans to the six stores daily, and is proud of the variety and fifty blends, roasts, and flavored coffees you'll find here. Noteworthy: Sulawesi Kalossi from Indonesia and Ethiopian Yrgacheff. But the best-seller is the house blend of French Roast Colombian and Sumatra coffees, consumed with shortbread, or a stroopwafel.

# Pasqua Coffee Bars

*Monday through Friday 7 A.M. to 5 P.M.*
For branches, call: 695-2800

PASQUA, A WEST COAST COFFEE CHAIN, has lots of branches in San Francisco and Los Angeles, and is now working on New York (there's a Pasqua at La Guardia, too). Design relies on copper counters, marble floors, and minimalism—off-white walls display a few black and white prints. Three coffees are sold: the six bean dark roast Pasqua Filter Blend, Decaf, and an Espresso. Nonfat latte shakes can also be made with banana. Low- and nonfat danishes star among the breakfast treats, and afternoons, there are pastries, lemon bars, crumb cake, and cookies. Note: Pasqua's beans, roasted in San Francisco, are sold within nine days of their arrival.

## Pax World

*Daily 6:30 A.M. to Midnight*
For branches, call: 664-1820

WE'RE NOT TALKING ATMOSPHERE HERE, unless it's the '90s fast-food version of an Italian-accented New York deli-cum-bakery. The premises glitter with white tile, chrome, and cleanliness, and seating, when available, leans to dark wood restaurant chairs and laminated tables. But volume ensures freshness, the full spectrum of Italian coffee drinks is available, and there are literally dozens of sweet treats to buy on impulse, from raspberry-glazed cheesecake to carrot cake, all larger and brighter than life.

## Starbucks

*Monday through Saturday 6 A.M. to Midnight; Sunday 7 A.M. to 11:30 P.M.*
For branches, call: 505-5175

IT SEEMS AS IF there's a Starbucks on every corner in the city, each one spacious, many-windowed, streamlined, gleaming with halogen lights, and fitted with pristine woodwork designed to display all the Starbucks stuff fans can't live without. Smooth, engineered surfaces and a palette based on the coffee bean seem a tad sterile, but recently-opened Starbucks strive for individuality. While some complain the chain overroasts its multitudinous coffees, it's fine by most New Yorkers.

# Timothy's World Coffee

*Monday through Friday 7 A.M. to 6 P.M.; Saturday 7 A.M. to 11 P.M.;*
*Sunday 7 A.M. to 7 P.M.*
For branches, call 644-2653

TIMOTHY'S COZY, European-style coffee bars, with the now-familiar rounded logo circled with flags, shun the high-tech look; the low-shine interiors are warmed with terra-cotta walls and brass-accented mahogany-tone wood; wainscoting adds a cheerful note. The thirty or more coffees dispensed from a curved, built-in bar include five to seven flavored beans. There's a good selection of sweet and light lunch options available: try a pumpkin muffin, honey-raisin scone, or a pear-raisin danish, perhaps. Besides the beans to go, Timothy's offers seven different hot chocolate mixes (hazelnut is excellent), plus iced teas and lemonades.

# Coffee
# at Retail/Mail
# Order

# Balducci's (R) (MO)

424 Sixth Ave. bet. 9th and 10th Sts.
New York, NY 10011 ~ 673-2600
*Daily 7 A.M. to 8:30 P.M.*

BALDUCCI'S HAS ALWAYS BEEN KNOWN—and loved—for its cramped maze of aisles and overwhelming dazzle of delicacies. Luckily, there is plenty of room for the coffee lover to browse amongst the brews because the shop has stashed its sixty-plus coffees way at the back, past the pasta, away from the hubbub. The tidy alcove, filled from floor to ceiling with beans, reveals a wide spectrum of hues from deep, almost pitch-black to pale brown. Burlap bags highlight roasts such as India Monsooned Malabar AA, Kenya Nyeri AA, and Yauco Selecto AA, among others. Best-sellers are the House Blend, French Roast, and Italian Espresso. Specialty decaffeinateds include Nina's A.M. and P.M. brews.

# Cafe 59 (R)

BLOOMINGDALE'S
1000 Third Ave. bet. E. 59th and 60th Sts. ~ 705-2000
*Monday through Friday 10 A.M. to 8:30 P.M.;*
*Saturday 10 A.M. to 7 P.M.; Sunday 11 A.M. to 7 P.M.*

CAFE 59 LIES ON EAST 59TH STREET, almost midway between the avenues. At rush hour, traffic shoots by, gears screaming, horns blasting on the way to the 59th Street Bridge. Be not afraid. Cafe 59 will sell you a decaf espresso to calm your nerves as you examine the almost twenty coffee bean dispensers which, in gleaming brass and glass, line one wall. French Roast is popular; so are Cappuccino and Viennese with Cinnamon. By the window there's an étagere stuffed with Bloomie's own gaily labeled bags of beans, including "Main Course" and "Decaf Kona Extra Fancy." "Chocolate Raspberry Truffle" sounds rich and fattening—but that's the beauty of coffee: it isn't.

## The Coffee Grinder (R) (MO)

348 E. 66th St. bet. First and Second Aves.
New York, NY 10021 ∼ 737-3490
*Monday through Friday 9:30 A.M. to 7 P.M.;*
*Saturday 9:30 A.M. to 6 P.M.*

AN INTIMATE, LIBRARY-LIKE EMPORIUM of coffees and teas, the Coffee Grinder has graced its upper East Side neighborhood for over twenty years. Look in the window: a gigantic cup and saucer sit smugly upon a leather-tufted chair surrounded by seasonal plants. A blackboard lists the forty coffees available by the scoop; shelves alongside the counter display prepackaged beans. The Coffee Grinder prides itself on blending mixes to a consumer's taste. Coffees to note are the Brazilian Santos, Colombian Excelsio, Costa Rican Tarazu, Ethiopian Moch, and Sumatra, among others. Accoutrements such as plunge pots and traditional Chemexes are complemented by a special series of New York mugs designed by Pat Singer, an artist who lives on this street. If you want to hang around, a table and chairs are on the sidewalk outside.

# Dean & Deluca (R) (MO)

560 Broadway bet. Prince and Spring Sts.
New York, NY 10012 ~ 431-1691
*Monday through Saturday 8 A.M. to 8 P.M.; Sunday 9 A.M. to 7 P.M.*

THE LUXE GOURMET EMPORIUM that is Dean & Deluca is so packed on weekends that it can be difficult, if not impossible, to contract with the bean vendor for your one-half pound of a favorite from among the three dozen beans on display in burlap sacks—especially if you want the beans ground to your specification as well. But persevere! D&D also sells an assortment of canned and bagged beans: Douwe Egberts, La Semeuse, Illy, and Danesi are represented, as are New Orleans's Cafe du Monde chicory and First Colony organics. At the back of the shop, coffee accoutrements are assembled: D&D's own mugs, of course, and tiny brown espresso cups, plus Bialetti's stainless-steel stovetop espresso pot and Pavoni's snazzy espresso maker available in two sizes. For the truly addicted, or those who need to get a buzz on before (or after) they dive into the aisles, D&D hosts a small, intensely sociable espresso bar just inside the front door. Check out the mail-order flyer, too.

# Eli's Bread & Vinegar Factory (R)

431 E. 91st St. bet. First and East End Aves. ∼ 987-0885
*Daily 7 A.M. to 9 P.M.*

FOR THOSE FAMILIAR with Eli Zabar's E.A.T. on Madison Avenue, and with his breads, the 91st Street block just west of the Asphalt Green is a delicious detour. Here, the Vinegar Factory swings open huge garage doors to an emporium abundant with gourmet foods. The beans, ranked at the southeast corner, right next to the breads, include Eli's House Blend; these are displayed for the customer to scoop and weigh, and grind if desired. Some beans are prepackaged in poly ziplocks. At the back of the store, surrounded by biscotti, cakes, tartes, pies, and cookies (all, naturally, baked on premises) is a coffee-to-go set-up. The Vinegar Factory recently opened an eatery on a balcony overlook. Go on up, have a bite, and scan the scene below.

# Empire Coffee & Tea Company (R) (MO)

592 Ninth Ave. bet. 42nd and 43rd Sts.
New York, NY 10036 ∼ 586-1717; 800-262-5908
231 Washington St., Hoboken, NJ 07030 ∼ 201-261-9625
*Monday through Friday 8 A.M. to 7 P.M.;*
*Saturday 9 A.M. to 6:30 P.M.; Sunday 11 A.M to 5 P.M.*

THE "EMPIRE" OF THE NAME might simply be short for empirical, for this no-frills emporium is nothing if not efficient. Although Empire operates a "Java Station" for coffee by the cup, its main purpose is to dispense beans by the pound, and to fulfill mail-order requests. Coffee wares include classic Melittas and Chemexes accompanied by unbleached paper or Swiss gold permanent filters, plus Bialetti stainless-steel stovetop espresso pots in the three-, six-, and nine-cup sizes.

## Fairway Fruits & Vegetables (R)

2127 Broadway bet. 74th and 75th Sts. ~ 595-1888
*Daily 7 A.M. to Midnight.*

YOU EITHER LOVE IT OR YOU HATE IT, but Fairway indubitably has its place in the city's psyche. Plaudits cite Fairway's incredible abundance of fresh vegetables, cheeses, baked goods—and coffees. If you're in search of the latter, plunge into the fray and head for the back of the store, savoring its Les Halles-like ambiance en route; sniff and eye the towering piles of gleaming fruits and produce. There are forty-four different coffees to browse, several of them nut- or spice-flavored. For something different, try the India Mysore, Bay City Roast, or the Brazil Estate.

## Grace's Marketplace (R)
1237 Third Ave. at 71st St. ∼ 737-0600
*Monday through Saturday 7 A.M. to 8:30 P.M.; Sunday 8 A.M. to 7 P.M.*

GRACE'S PURVEYS over three-dozen varieties of coffee bean, plus another dozen decafs, in a pleasant alcove shared with a colorful assortment of gourmet jelly beans and nuts. A few stovetop espresso makers are displayed on shelves over the beans; particularly handy are the little Vespresso one–cup and the Benjamin & Medwin brand four-cup. Other brands include Junior and Kontessa. The grinder carried here is the Grindmaster "caffemill." Coffee in one-pound cans from Illy, Lavazza. Caffe Kimbo and Danesi are also available.

## Hadleigh's (R)
1900 Broadway bet. 63rd and 64th Sts. ∼ 580-0669
*Monday through Saturday 6:30 A.M. to 9 P.M.; Sunday 7:30 A.M. to 8 P.M.*

LOCATED ACROSS FROM LINCOLN CENTER, Hadleigh's is a friendly European-style emporium of specialty foods where luxurious name brands, such as Maxim's of Paris—with its own distinctive tin of coffee, Maxim Pur Arabica d'Exception—stand out. (Hadleigh's also carries Lavazza and Le Semeuse.) Wide aisles and user-friendly displays make shopping here a real pleasure. Three-dozen varieties of bean are ranked behind the counter; if you want to stay and sip one of the roasts of the day, there is a cheerful clutch of tables up front near the windows, and, for one intimate couple, a single table cozily snuggled up against the oils and cheeses in the deli section towards the back. Of the cakes on display in the pastry case, the chocolate chip caught our eye.

# Macy's (R)

THE CELLAR

151 W. 34th St. at Herald Square  ~  695-4400

*Monday, Thursday, and Friday 10 A.M. to 8:30 P.M.; Tuesday, Wednesday, and Saturday 10 A.M. to 7 P.M.; Sunday 11 A.M. to 7 P.M.*

MACY'S BOASTS that you can choose from more than sixty varieties of coffee beans and blends here in their New York "coffee head-quarters." Coffee shares an enclave with an abundance of tempting gourmet packaged cookies, from La Tempesta to Effie Marie's. Here is hard-to-find Caravali Coffee—try the Guatemala Antigua with its smoky, distinctive flavor. Browse the assortment of First Colony beans, displayed in more than sixty acrylic dispensers bracketing the counter area. Macy's own one and a half-pound vacuum packs offer good value, and there are charming coffee-brick theme gift packs: for your favorite golfer (if you have one), "Pro Choice" offers coffees with names like "Sandtrap Roast" and "Putter's Blend."

# McNulty's Tea & Coffee Co., Inc. (R) (MO)

109 Christopher St. bet. Hudson and Bleecker Sts.
New York, NY 10014 ~ 242-5351
*Monday through Saturday 10 A.M. to 9 P.M.; Sunday 1 A.M. to 7 P.M.*

ONE OF THE OLDEST PURVEYORS of coffee in this city, McNulty's—in operation since 1895—carries, and mail-orders, almost one hundred different types of coffee. Ten-pound burlap sacks of various blends are stenciled with their contents and are stacked inside the door and beside the counter; others are displayed in jars. Coffees include specialty blends with names such as "William and Mary," "Toltec," and "Old Judge's." Prices range from $8.40 per pound for basic blends to $24 for more rare Jamaican Blue Mountain. Most fall within the $8.40 to $10.95 range. Shelving behind the counter displays an array of non-electric coffee makers, including the "Junior" cafetiere in three sizes, Melittas and filters, and the classic French plunge pot.

# Porto Rico Importing Company (R)

40 1/2 St. Mark's Pl. bet. First and Second Aves. ~ 533-1982
201 Bleecker St. bet. Sixth Ave. and MacDougal St. ~ 477-5421
107 Thompson St. bet. Prince and Spring Sts. ~ 966-5758
*Monday through Saturday 9 A.M. to 9 P.M.; Sunday Noon to 7 P.M.*

THE VERY INSOUCIANCE of the St. Mark's Place coffee dispensary sets it apart from its more no-nonsense alter-ego in the West Village and the former Auggie's in SoHo. Salespeople of the youthful nose-ring variety toss in plenty of bon mots with the beans. Coffees—over eighty varieties—are artistically collected in open, plastic-lined burlap bags. Shelves display a panoply of coffee makers, from the magnificent, gleaming copper-and-brass espresso machine known as "Il Futuro" to more modest Chemexes and Melittas, with their companion filters. Bodum's "Chambord" plunger is here, as well as its "Bistro" baby.

## The Sensuous Bean (R)

66 W. 70th St. bet. Central Park West and Columbus Ave. ∼ 724-7725

*Monday, Thursday, and Friday 10 A.M. to 9 P.M.; Tuesday and Wednesday 10 A.M. to 7 P.M.; Saturday 9:30 A.M. to 7 P.M.; Sunday 11 A.M. to 6 P.M.*

THIS PLACE IS FUN—full of beans, in fact. If you like the idea of mix 'n' match blends to your own fancy, this is where you can indulge your palate and take a "be your own barista" approach to coffee. The long-established Sensuous Bean carries dozens of coffees—light, medium, and dark roasts, and Swiss water process decafs. Flavored coffees are imaginative: add a little Seville Orange to a French Roast for a dessert treat. Coffees are kept in small wood barrels collared in jute and sealed with acrylic lids that bear the bean or blend name and description. Along with four heroic/Heath Robinson coffee bean grinders (one reserved for flavored coffee only), they constitute the decor. Six vacuum thermoses dispense coffee and three glass jars of biscotti complete take-out options. Industrial shelving jammed up against the window offers teas, honey, fruit butters, and cookies.

## Two for the Pot (R)

200 Clinton St., Brooklyn ~ 718-855-8173
*Tuesday through Friday Noon to 7 P.M.; Saturday 10 A.M. to 6 P.M.*

OWNER JOHN MCGILL opened Two for the Pot in 1973, and there's very little he doesn't know about coffee (or for that matter, teas, herbs and spices). He buys beans from five different roasters. Depending on the time of year, Two for the Pot offers between three- and four-dozen different beans and blends. You'll find a selection of organic coffees, both regular and decaf, and two dozen regular coffees, which include McGill's house blend, a full-bodied blend of Colombian, Guatemalan, and Costa Rica beans, with a touch of dark roast. There's also a New Orleans-style blend with a strong chicory presence that's as authentic as anything you might hope to find in Louisiana, and a wonderful Kona from Hawaii. If you'd like to create your own blend, McGill will lend his expertise to the cause.

# Zabar's (R)

2245 Broadway bet. 80th and 81st Sts.  787-2000
*Monday through Friday 8 A.M. to 7:30 P.M.;*
*Saturday 8 A.M. to 10 P.M.; Sunday 9 A.M. to 6 P.M.*

THERE'S ALWAYS A LOGJAM OF CARTS and elbowing shoppers around Zabar's "coffee department," where sacks of beans and stacks of coffee in the store signature orange-and-white bags create an impression of circled wagons, from behind which beleaguered sales people weigh, grind, and bag as fast as they can. Zabar's buys its beans green in huge quantities, and has them custom-roasted to its specifications, selling up to 1,500 pounds weekly of ten or so basic coffees. The house blend is perhaps the most popular; others include Colombian, Kona style, Blue Mountain style, Continental and Swiss blends. Then there are dark roasts: French-Italian, Vienna and a Dark French Roast. There are also three decaf coffees. Note: Zabar's roasts on the light side to emphasize flavor over body.

# Index by Neighborhood

# About the Authors

BO NILES is an editor and writer who specializes in design and decoration. She is a contributing editor to *Country Living* magazine and the author of a number of books including *White by Design* and *Living with Lace*.

VERONICA MCNIFF is an arts administrator and freelance writer specializing in the decorative arts. Her articles are published in a number of magazines including *House Beautiful* and *Travel & Leisure*.

# About the Illustrator

SUSAN COLGAN is a painter whose still lives are published in *Among Flowers,* a collaboration with poet Susan Kinsolving. She lives and works in New York and Berkshire County, Massachusetts.

BO NILES AND VERONICA MCNIFF are the co-authors of *The New York Book of Tea,* illustrated by SUSAN COLGAN, and published by CITY & COMPANY.